Di'lshad.

972-800-0712

Rules of Engagement

Making Connections Last

Froswa' Booker-Drew

Rules of Engagement: Making Connections Last

Author: Froswa' Booker-Drew

Published by Austin Brothers Publishing
Fort Worth, Texas

www.austinbrotherspublishing.com

ISBN: 978-0-9891027-0-4

Cover Design by Jay Cookingham

This and other books published by
Austin Brothers Publishing
can be purchased at -
www.austinbrotherspublishing.com

Printed in the United States of America
2013 -- First Edition

"*Women fare better where civic engagement is greater, and they fare worse where people are isolated and disconnected from their communities. Engaging more women in civic and political participation may be a crucial tool for advancing their status more generally—and improving women's status may be important to improving the overall civic health of the country.*"

(Caizza and Putnam, 2002)

"*If you want one year of prosperity, grow grain. If you want ten years of prosperity, grow trees. If you want one hundred years of prosperity, grow people.*"

(Chinese proverb)

Contents

Acknowledgements

When my publisher suggested a tree on the cover of the book, I wasn't really sure if that would relay the message I wanted for this book. Then he reminded me of a quote that I have in the signature line of my email, "If you want one year of prosperity, grow grain. If you want ten years of prosperity, grow trees. If you want one hundred years of prosperity, grow people." (Chinese proverb)

The aforementioned quote is the epitome of what this book is about. It is designed to help individuals grow through self-awareness and building positive, high-quality connections that ultimately transform individual lives, families, organizations, and communities.

This workbook for women has been a labor of love. While writing this book, I have been a mother, wife, daughter, relative, friend, leader, mentor, student, and teacher. Juggling multiple relationships that have sown into my life has finally made this dream a reality.

I am forever grateful to my husband Charles and daughter Kazai who have shared me with so many others. They listened endlessly about my aspirations and concerns. Even though my time was limited, they loved and encouraged me to soar. I LOVE YOU BOTH!!!!

My mother, Dorothy Booker-Petterway, is an amazing woman who has been my rock. I am blessed to have a mother that I not only admire and adore but one who is my best friend and biggest cheerleader. Much love to my family fan club who are present at EVERY honor, event, and anything I do: my stepfather James Petterway, aunts Teresa Pinkney-

Toliver and Beatrice Hardy and family, Uncle Mac (Joe Mc-Gaskey), Kim McGaskey-Jones and family, and my BFFs, Lillian Calhoun and Deirdre Phillips.

My research group, who are more than guinea pigs but my dear friends, you were the inspiration for this project turning into a book: Emily Vernon (who also gave input to the book and so much valuable insight), Mona Kafeel, Michelle Accardo, Dana Fay, Wende Burton, Debra Levy, Brittany Barnett, and Dawn Granger.

To my Antioch family—Cohort 10 and faculty—this journey has been an exceptional one because of your insightful dialogue, brilliance, and support. I have learned so much because of each of you. Special thanks to my advisor, Laurien Alexandre for holding me accountable and your vote of confidence in me from day one as a PhD student.

Carolyn Wright, Carl Millender, Kimberly Pitts, Shellye and Cedric Lyons, Lucia Retta—for your extra eyes, feedback, questions, and belief in this project and in me.

Terry Austin, publisher, for giving me a chance and taking so much time and effort to make this into something special.

Sue Sullins and the cast/crew of *Friendly Captivity*—the experience that sowed the seed for my desire to help women.

Dr. Terry Flowers, my mentor and friend....I am forever grateful!

Greg Campbell who encouraged me to write a book and go back to school for years!

Rafael Munoz, Comfort Brown, and Ingra Green for being my cheerleaders on and off the clock.

Arnie Adkinson—thanks for being a supervisor that offered me the flexibility to grow and go.

The list of supporters is lengthy and if I've left anyone out, please know it is a function of my aging brain and not my loving heart.

Introduction

*M*ost of us have attended networking events with the hopes of meeting people to connect with for either professional or personal reasons. However, after you have exchanged numerous business cards and made promises to call each other the next day, you are met with the disappointment of that potential connection not returning your calls or emails. In actuality, most people define networking as only exchanging cards and information. This hit me one day as I attended what was supposed to be one the best networking events in the area. It was definitely well attended and I could see that people were armed and ready to distribute business cards.

As I was preparing to be approached, I could not help but think how people in the room felt that sharing a business card was real networking. Your business card lists your name, what you do, your title, and your contact information. It doesn't share who you really are and it certainly doesn't compel others to work with you. Your card is just a form of contact that provides a description of your vocation and a location. However, many people rely on this as their networking tool.

I was one of those people for a long time. However, through my experiences over the last several years I have had the opportunity to travel to a number of places domestically and internationally. I have met amazing college students, scores of electric, engaging people in my pursuit of my doctorate while being a professor and through my work in non-profit management. I have met people who have influenced my life. With all these interactions and connections, I have learned what authentic, realistic, and strategic networking is about. Through tried and true methods, I have learned that networking is your personal responsibility. It is up to you to develop and maintain the connections you make. Additionally, your character and who you are influences the depths of your connections and relationships. We will delve into this throughout the book.

This book will illustrate to you a new paradigm shift in networking. Gone are the days of giving out business cards with the hopes of creating a new relationship. Gone are the days that your place of employment or your position will open the doors for you. Authentic networking is built on personal and professional interactions. The principles we will outline in this book will help you establish a networking system that is authentic and customized to who you are. We will share nuggets of knowledge about networking that will become a part of your everyday life. I venture to believe that you are reading this book for the very reason I outlined. You want a change and you desire stronger relationships.

The book is built around three types of relationship capital (see diagram) – Identity Capital, Psychological Capital, and Social Capital. In order to build healthy, lasting networks, all three are crucial. We will describe each type of capital and then offer "rules of engagement" that provide guidelines for building your capacity for connecting with others.

You will notice a stark difference in this book from typical networking books. **This is not a book designed to be read all at once. It might seem repetitive at times, but that is intentional in order to reinforce various concepts.**

The chapters are designed to be read daily, if not weekly, so that you have time to process the information and make it real in your life. I am a firm believer that in order to create lasting and meaningful relationships you have to be aware of who you are and cognizant of issues that can hinder relationship building. You need to have a mindset to build your

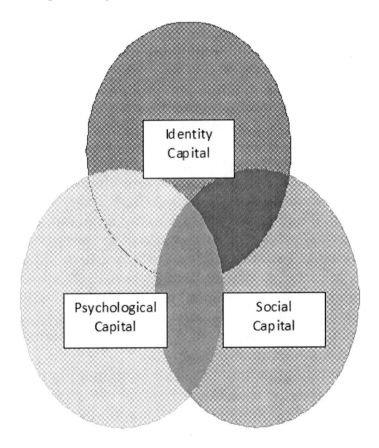

Although human capital is important, based on my research, I recognized that all three of these were at work when women discussed relationships and the ability to connect to others.

capacity for connecting with your personal and professional contacts. Productive and genuine networking is a matter of personal decision.

Let me get back to the experience I was sharing about a networking event. A beautifully dressed and polished woman walked toward me. I wondered what this connection might yield. Before this potential customer/business associate or possibly new acquaintance said hello, I knew immediately the first question that was going to be asked. She stretched out her hand, said hello, and then asked me what I did for a living. I just sighed inside. She did not introduce herself. She wasn't interested in my journey and how our paths might connect to create or collaborate. So I responded to her question because you never know what the conversation could potentially offer in creating impactful results.

Then the next question I knew was coming was whether I liked my work. It was at that point I knew I passed the initial test. What I shared with her interested her enough to stay to talk. Sadly this example is what so many people view as networking. People want to see if what you do will somehow help or support their particular interest or goals. Unfortunately that is not genuine networking. Truth be told, she could have had the best services and offerings but because there was no connection we both would never know what could have been a great collaboration.

As I often would sit in my office, baffled as to why people attend events but not intend to really make a connection, I came up with two conclusions. First, many people do not know how to authentically create professional relationships that can have lasting results. Second, there is a level of responsibility that comes in creating genuine and long lasting relationships. In my pursuit of answering these questions, I was led me down an exciting but interesting journey as I talked to people from all walks of life about what they define as networking and relationship building.

As we journey through this book about the rules of engagement, I am going to share with you relationships that have impacted my life, lessons I have learned, and some principles that you can use when creating your network. I've been fortunate to have had some wonderful relationships in my life that have shaped and developed who I am. My first key relationship was with my mother. My mother, to this day, is my biggest cheerleader. She has always been honest, insightful, and yet, blunt to a fault but I knew that even in those moments of firmness, she taught me how to love. Relationships that existed early in our lives play a role in how we view ourselves and the way we connect to others.

Foundation for Connecting

My mother taught me when building relationships, whether personal or professional, to always start with honesty, be open to people regardless of their background, and to be a person that others know they can trust. Whether you have a mother, sister, aunt, grandmother, or whomever you deem as special to you, think about that first important relationship in your life. Reflect on what that person has taught you. What did you learn from them about life, how to treat others, how to build relationships, or even how to grow as a person? Reflecting on that first relationship is the first step in the Rules of Engagement.

One of the biggest challenges we face as a society is how we connect to others. Relationships are critical, not only in our personal lives but also our professional lives. One thing is clear, people are different but we all have a desire to be connected with someone who gives our life meaning and compliments our purpose.

In contrast to my mother, my relationship with my father wasn't always the best. Growing up I was like every other young girl, I wanted to have that special father and daughter bond. It is often said that a woman's view of men is formed by the example that her father sets. When I was a little girl, my father was a giant to me. At six feet six inches tall, he towered over everyone. He evoked this feeling of security, like when he held my hands when walking to school I felt like my world was safe. Anything I may have been experiencing at school seemed to fade on the journey while we walked together. That was a feeling I wanted to keep and never have uprooted.

When I was six years old, I was a daddy's girl who enjoyed being around him and absorbing his huge presence. One day I decided to sit on my dad's lap like I had always done. But this day was different. He told me abruptly to get off, no explanation or reason given and no emotion. He told me to get off his lap and that was it. I thought I had done something wrong. As I stood there hoping for a reason, I was standing face to face with my first lesson in experiencing rejection.

I didn't know until I was much older why he asked me to move. He felt I was growing up and it wasn't appropriate for a little girl to sit on her father's lap. I just thought it was something wrong with me. It wasn't until I was an adult that I realized how this first memory impacted so many of my relationships, especially with men. At that very moment, that situation changed how I saw my hero.

To some people this may not seem life changing, but for a six-year-old girl it was major. I was rejected by my father, my strong hero and didn't know why. I didn't properly deal with the issue of rejection and pain because without an explanation, I was not able to have closure. This changed the dynamic of our relationship.

It now makes sense why I struggled for so much of my life seeking connections that validated me. For many of us, we seek the approval from others because of the rejection we encountered from someone who meant something to us. Our first major life lesson can have a strong effect on how we build and maintain our future relationships. Bill Crawford once said, "Our past is not, as some fear, a series of events carved in stone that we must carry around for the rest of our lives... but a kaleidoscope of experiences that, when viewed through different lenses, can 'color' (change) how we see our present and future."

These experiences can impede our ability to connect with others and we miss out on real opportunities to move beyond the pain to find possibilities. If we are not careful, these experiences jade us from making valuable connections. Life serves as a laboratory, allowing us an opportunity to create and implement new strategies that work. You can mix different types of people, from all walks of life, and different experiences and backgrounds. If you put them all in a room you never know what will be generated as a result of the interactions. It is simply fascinating to me because the possibilities of creating great networks from different groups of people will yield more connections, a greater reach, and more opportunities to grow. Yet, so many people do not fully appreciate this principle. We often search for people who are in our same industry, attended the same type of schools, have similar friends, or who have similar goals. Think about how often you have started your day with the mindset that you want to intentionally meet people that are drastically different from you. It is not common practice but it is one that can yield a new perspective on relationships and add to your network.

I've been fortunate to have had so many experiences that have provided a foundation for my interactions. My friends call me a master networker and although I have been blessed to meet and have a variety of networks, I am more concerned about relationships and not just having a stack of business cards or thousands of Facebook friends. I am genuinely interested in the individual and how our journeys have intersected for a reason.

Stewardship is a word that is used significantly in the nonprofit world especially as it relates to funding. Cultivating and maintaining relationships with donors is critical for a nonprofit organization's success. As leaders in our homes, on our jobs, and in our communities, stewarding relationships is necessary.

Just as we take care of our gardens, our homes, our bodies, and our cars, we must do the same in our relationships. I use the analogy of a garden because when you want a beautiful garden it is important to till the soil, plant the seeds, and water them. One day you have a beautiful harvest. Sowing seeds of your time, energy, resources, and commitment can reap a harvest of great relationships and connections.

As I complete my PhD at Antioch University, my learning lab has been working with a group of women who have taught me about building relationships and the importance of opportunities to be real. Over the course of four months, I met with nine women for two to three hours monthly to discuss their experiences concerning social capital.

The women ranged in age from late twenties to early fifties. They represented various ethnic, racial, religious, socioeconomic statuses, educational levels ranging from a returning college student to a recent graduate of the bar exam. One was a nonprofit executive and another was a stay at home/scholar-activist mom. They were single, in the process of going through a divorce, married (happily and with challenges), or engaged. Some were not mothers, others had young children, a few had adult children, and even one had given up her child for adoption as a college student. Their experiences were wildly different—coming from a life of extreme poverty to experiencing privilege. Our monthly meetings were filled with laughter, tears, shock, and awe. Regardless of their situations, what they had in common was their desire to connect, share, and learn.

They taught me that all of us desire connection and relationships that matter. I realized it is more than the exchange of resources for those I studied and listened to. It was really about an opportunity to give, grow, and share of themselves in a space that allowed them to be authentic and transparent. Many are stressed because we do not have relationships that fulfill and complement our existence. Most relationships drain us to the very core and are not mutually satisfying. What was even more profound is that a couple of the women did not even realize the void they were feeling until they became a part of this group. Even as we approached our last group meeting, they asked for more opportunities to be together. Once you build a network in your own life you will see how fiercely you don't want to see it leave. It is through their experiences and my ability to eavesdrop on their conversations that I wrote my thoughts and observations.

This book is a small glimpse of what I have learned from these women and from my experiences in building relationships. Initially, I expected the women would share their relationships to help one another. I realized that more than social capital was exchanged. These women shared psychological capital and enlightened each of us as to how their experiences formed their identity. Participants read assignments and completed evaluations at the close of each session. Dialogue themes from each of the sessions have been used in the design of this handbook.

I have come up with twenty-nine engagement rules that I believe are critical for building social, psychological, and identity capital in your life. Walk with me as I share details about what each of these mean and how they can apply to your life. This isn't so much a book to tell you what to do but more to provide an opportunity for thinking about what is important in your life as you grow. All of us want to become stronger in our personal and professional lives which are filled daily with interactions with others.

Before we move forward into more of the various engagement principles, I want you to think about what your professional/personal image is communicating. I'm not referring to what you choose to wear. That is important but not in the context of what I am referencing here. When we talk about creating networks and building relationships, we have to be the type of person that someone wants to connect to.

ACTION POINT

List three situations and/or times when you were the most happy in your life. In each instance, what elements were present when I felt that way? How was I feeling about myself during those times?

_____

_____

_____

_____

_____

_____

Beginning when I was a child, what are the 10 most significant events in my life? Why did I make them significant? What period of my life do I like most? Why? What period of my life do I like least? Why?

_____

_____

_____

_____

_____

Identity Capital

I find, as I try to become a better person, I rely heavily on the wisdom of my mother and others who have lived longer. I also find that books like the Bible are important in providing guidance. One of my favorite scriptures is "Love your neighbor as you love yourself" (Mark 12:31 GNT). I am in awe that we spend so much time on the first part of this statement. It is important to love your neighbor. But how is it possible to demonstrate love to others when the love we should have for ourselves is lacking? If we don't love ourselves, those around us will receive the same treatment. The connection we have to ourselves is reflected in how we treat others.

I read an impactful article by Laura Morgan Roberts, called *Creating a Positive Professional Image*. I wanted to include excerpts because it offered a different approach to professional and personal image. Asking yourself the questions below will encourage you to examine the way you interact with others and how you develop your relationships on a daily basis.

"Your professional image is the set of qualities and characteristics that represent perceptions of your competence and character as judged by your key constituents (i.e., clients, superiors, subordinates, colleagues)…First, you must realize that if you aren't managing your own professional image, someone else is. People are constantly observing your behavior and forming theories about your competence, character, and commitment, which are rapidly disseminated throughout your workplace. It is only wise to add your voice in framing others' theories about who you are and what you can accomplish."[1]

She furthers encourages us to be the author of our own identity. Take a strategic, proactive approach to managing your image:

Identify your ideal state.
- What are the core competencies and character traits you want people to associate with you?
- Which of your social identities do you want to emphasize and incorporate into your workplace interactions, and which would you rather minimize?

Assess your current image, culture, and audience.
- What are the expectations for professionalism?
- How do others currently perceive you?

Conduct a cost-benefit analysis for image change.
- Do you care about others' perceptions of you?
- Are you capable of changing your image?
- Are the benefits worth the costs? (Cognitive, psychological, emotional, physical effort)

Use strategic self-presentation to manage impressions and change your image. Pay attention to the balancing act—build credibility while maintaining authenticity.

Manage the effort you invest in the process.
- Monitoring others' perceptions of you
- Monitoring your own behavior

---

1   Laura Roberts, "Creating a Positive Professional Image" *Working Knowledge: The Thinking that Leads.* Harvard Business School, 20 06 2005. Web. 6 Mar 2013. <http://hbswk.hbs.edu/item/4860.html>.

- Strategic self-disclosure
- Preoccupation with proving worth and legitimacy

If you were asked to describe who you were, what would you say? Would you share about your career, home life, personal interests, or your volunteer activities? Knowing your identity is key. Identity capital is about knowing yourself and understanding that who you are shapes how you approach relationships. Each of us has a story. Each of us has something we can share with others. When we

> *How you treat others is a reflection of how you truly feel about yourself.*

aren't clear on our story, then our triggers, those things that have influenced who we are and shape our perspectives, can make it difficult to appreciate the stories of others. Knowing your purpose helps you to understand how others can intersect and be a part of your journey.

When you are aware of your hopes and dreams, when setbacks occur (and they do) you are able to endure because you have the emotional, spiritual, and mental support to move forward. You are then able to find others who can serve as support and provide the positive affirmation and energy you need to make progress. Once you know who you are and where you are going, you can then build connections that matter. Although academic circles use the term social capital, authentic networking actually is more than just an exchange for personal gain and benefit. It is about everyone benefiting from the relationship. It is more than a completed transactions. It is about transformation.

Evelyn is an African American female in her early 50's. She is the mother of four adult children and a grandmother of one. Married to her children's father for a number of years, she endured significant challenges in the relationship. Her husband had a strong addiction to drugs that ended their relationship. This new chapter of her life helped her make the decision to move her small children across the country to start a new life.

Evelyn credits her ability to navigate through her struggles as a result of her strong sense of faith, which has shaped her identity. Often, trials and the pressures of life cause you to find an inner strength that you do not realize you possess. Through experiences you grow, learn, and attract life lessons that are designed to propel you to the next level. Since Evelyn had a strong sense of self combined with an understanding of the many life lessons she experienced, she attracted healthier business relationships and long lasting friendships that have been intact for a number of years.

She was able to share her struggles with the group without feeling embarrassed and felt those difficulties were an opportunity to connect to others. Her honesty and self-disclosure brought the group together and created opportunities for others to share their stories. Evelyn offers a glimpse into the importance of self-discovery and awareness as an opportunity to understand and connect with others when one is authentic and transparent. This leads us to the definition of identity capital.

ACTION POINT

What type of people do I enjoy spending time with? (intelligent, open-minded, outgoing, self-righteous, reflective, quiet, funny, a bit sad, optimists, readers, pessimists, thinkers, sports-minded, active, perceptive, debaters, joke-tellers, etc.)

Why do I enjoy those specific qualities in people?

_____

_____

_____

Do I seek out people similar to myself or different from me?
Why is that?

_____

_____

_____

_____

Do I have many friends as I just described? Why or why not?

_____

_____

_____

_____

How many close friends do I want based on the amount of
time I have?

_____

_____

_____

What would those close relationships look like? What would be the biggest aspects? (talking, shared activities, working on projects together, laughter, storytelling, playing games, etc.)

_____

_____

_____

_____

What is the single biggest attitudinal change I'd like to make when I'm with people? (be more myself, be more out-going, be more honest, initiate more conversations, be more comfortable, be more open, be funnier, interrupt less, initiate more activities, etc.)

_____

_____

_____

_____

_____

My mother was raised by a single mother in poverty in Louisiana. If you are a single mother or know one, you are aware there are many challenges in raising children alone. What my grandmother taught my mother was invaluable. She walked her through what it meant to be a mother, a woman of integrity, and a woman that relies on God and family. This is what my mother instilled in me. Her experiences were a result of life encounters that formed and shaped her. We often take for granted how the experiences, both good and bad, impact who we are and our relationships with others. I realize my mother's experiences with women really impacted her view and how she approached certain situations.

What you were taught about relationship building, networking, communication, and any other life skills tends to be something you share with your colleagues. It is imperative to pay attention to what you have been taught. If your experiences, knowledge, and skill sets are not producing the desired results, you need to develop a new paradigm informed by new thinking about yourself and your values.

ACTION POINT

How you treat others is a reflection of how you truly feel about yourself. If you really want to challenge yourself, ask three to five people from your life how they feel you treat them. These should be people that will be honest with you. Match what they share with you with how you view yourself. Often in business, we ask this question in 360 degree evaluations but why not engage in the same discussions around both your personal and professional life? List the people you choose:

_____

_____

_____

_____

I am intrigued with many ideas. Identity capital is very important because as a mother raising a preteen daughter, I am watching my child develop an understanding of who she is and her place in the world. So many factors contribute to the development of who we are and how we see ourselves in comparison to others. Identity capital is based on how much time an individual contributes to their self-development. Identity is formed by culture, social structure, interaction, and personality. Our families, the media, socio-economic class, exposure, opportunities to connect, and the way in which we are wired all play a critical role in our development.

In our formative years, especially as teens, we begin to develop the way in which we will live. Life consistently presents challenges and opportunities. The way we address these challenges and opportunities can play a part in who we are and how we cope in the years to come. In essence, how we deal internally will impact the external. "Higher levels of ego strength help the person undertake more challenging tasks that can lead to greater future personal and economic benefits, and a greater sense of purpose in life facilitates long-term planning, increasing the likelihood of accomplishing higher-order personal and professional goals."[2] Perseverance to endure can result in achievement.

For many, the way we see ourselves is based on where we went to school, how much money we make or would like to make, the organizations we belong to, or our standing in the community. One of the conversations that resonated with many of the women in my research group was this idea of being "fake" or an imposter. One of the participants recalled going to a job she dreaded every day knowing that she really wanted to do something else. Another participant stated that this conversation was a moment of clarity for her. She had

---

2   J.E. Cote & S.J. Schwartz (2002) "Comparing psychological and sociological approaches to identity: identity status, identity capital, and the individualization process" Journal of Adolescence, 25, p. 574.

felt alone until that discussion. She realized that although many of her peers wanted to make partner at the firm, that wasn't her desire. It was this conversation that made her feel that she didn't have to follow suit. She could see this event in her life as a stepping stone to something greater and it wasn't a denial of who she really was, what was important, and her own personal truth.

How often do many of us wake up every morning denying the internal voice that cries out for something greater? We become a part of the status quo, forgetting our needs and what is truly important because we have lost our ability to hear the inner voice that serves as a guide. When was the last time that you found yourself in a situation that you desperately wanted to get out of but didn't?

Evaluate all the reasons you choose not to change that job, leave the relationship, pursue a business relationship, or even change the friendship. Imagine if you had someone in your life who could relate to your story. Would your situation change as a result of this interaction? Is it possible that the more opportunities we have to share and learn that others have similar experiences that we could actually strengthen us to move forward and make different decisions?

Often, we go through the routine of each day not paying attention to our own triggers and life lessons. A funny quote I've seen says, "Wherever you go, there you are." We don't realize that the direction we are headed is a clear indicator of the decisions we've made over the years. It is the recognition of your life story that is important because it serves as a foundation for your future success. Just as you've arrived at your current destination, you have the ability to change direction. But in order to do so, accessing your past and current location is essential. The stories that create your journey can shed light on why we achieve or struggle in various areas of our lives. It can even reveal why we have the connections with friends, significant others, and family that we do.

Psychological Capital

Psychological capital has its roots in organizational development and leadership theories. The focus in the past has been on traditional economic capital (what you have) and human capital (what you know) but you are also urged to look at who you are (psychological capital).[3]

There are four positive psychological capabilities which consist of confidence, hope, optimism, and resilience. Positive psychological capital is "....characterized by having confidence (self-efficacy) to take on and put in the necessary effort to succeed at challenging tasks, making positive attribution (optimism) about succeeding now and in the future, persevering toward goals and when necessary, redirecting paths to goals (hope) in order to succeed, and when beset by problems and adversity, sustaining and bouncing back and even beyond (resilience) to attain success."[4] In essence, when we have a positive view of life, we are able to deal with the challenges that we may encounter on our journey.

Efficacy is about your internal ability to create a plan to deal with whatever situation you might face. The way a per-

---

3   F. Luthans, K.W. Luthans, & B.C. Luthans (2004). "Positive Psychological Capital: Beyond Human And Social Capital" Business Horizons, 47(1), pp. 45-50.

4   *Ibid*, p. 46.

son deals with events in their life is in direct correlation to their efficacy. Those who feel defeated and believe they don't have the resources to make a difference have low efficacy. Individuals with high efficacy believe they have the ability and resources to address the challenges they are dealing with at the time.

Optimism "is associated with a positive outlook but is not an unchecked process without realistic evaluation. Hope consists of both will power and determination to achieve their goals and 'way power' thinking (being able to devise alternative pathways and extenuating plans to achieve a goal in the face of obstacles)."[5]

Individuals who are resilient have the ability to deal with stressors and "are open to new experiences, flexible to changing demands, and show more emotional stability when faced with adversity."[6] Setting goals and developing resources and skills, provide options to move forward instead of feeling stuck and defeated.

My faith walk is paramount in my journey; it is tied to my identity capital. Although I am aware that everyone has their own belief system, having a personal relationship with Christ has been such an important part of my life. My belief system serves as a compass when deciding what tasks I take on, what relationships I pursue or accept, and how I see myself. It is about a lifestyle of daily trying to be a better person based on Christ as my guide to fulfill my God given purpose.

I realize that everyone makes a decision on the path they choose. I am respectful of those choices that are different than my own. In my experience, people that don't accept others based on their personal value decisions lose out on potentially rewarding relationships and experiences. Under-

5   J.M. Avey, F. Luthans, & S.M. Jensen (2009) "Psychological Capital: A Positive Resource for Combating Employee Stress and Turnover" Human Resource Management, 48(5), p. 681.

6   *Ibid.*

standing my spiritual connection is more important than anything. My purpose in living is tied to how I am viewed by my Creator.

Since we are building a relationship of understanding through this book, I want to spend a little time sharing with you how I developed my understanding about the importance of a plan and the value of understanding we are designed for a purpose.

"Before I created you in the womb, I knew you; before you were born I set you apart...." (Jeremiah 1:5). I really believe that God has a design for our lives from the beginning. Sadly, our decisions and the decisions of others can impact the implementation of the purpose. When our purposes are affected, it can deter the types of relationships we can build.

As humans, we have the ability to make choices that affect our lives and those choices can directly or indirectly impact others. If I make a decision to consciously help you start your own business, I am choosing to invest my time, resources, and skills in you. If I choose to help you go to that next level in your professional life, then I am choosing to connect you to the best resources that will elevate your professional career. By choosing to sow into others, I am affecting the type of seeds that I will produce in my life and in those around me.

I remember when I was preparing to go to India, I asked a friend how she was able to keep her faith in God and not be angry at God for allowing the pain and suffering I knew I would encounter. She told me that God may have allowed these things to occur but man was responsible for the greed and suffering that existed in the world. Our choices throughout the years result in what exists today. As a Christian, I believe God calls us to greatness and in our own circle of influence we have the power to create positive change.

This is the basis of the rules of engagement: Everything we need to make a strong connection and build healthier professional and personal relationships is within us. Even if we have made choices that were not always in our best interest, we still have the ability to become our own personal change agent.

In my life I have been wounded often, especially in business relationships. Individuals I trusted to work with me often took ideas and advice and instead of including me, they chose to take those ideas and move on. There is a young lady in one of the classes that I teach who acknowledged that she has issues with bringing others into her circle. She is afraid that they will steal her ideas and as a result she struggles to grow the organization into the first class entity that it could become because of her past experiences with others. Often, unforgiveness blocks us from receiving the relationships that we want to experience.

Think about a time when someone hurt you in a professional and/or personal relationship. How has that wound impacted your ability to move forward? I have realized in my own experience that we all create walls. The challenge is coming to an understanding when those walls begin to create barriers for your own growth. How do you forgive those who have hurt you so that you do not use that pain to block future possibilities? When we think about pain, it can serve as a source of conflict or a source of catapulting us into our success.

In essence, when we have a positive view of life, we are able to deal with the challenges we may encounter on our journey. When you have a healthy outlook of life, you will find that you tend to look for opportunities that will enhance your personal and professional life. You wake up each day expecting great things to occur or with the intention that regardless of what happens you will choose to be content.

ACTION POINT

Reflect on those professional or personal situations that have hurt you:
What did you learn?

_____

_____

_____

_____

_____

_____

Did the pain hinder or help you? In what way?

_____

_____

_____

_____

How does it inform your decisions?

_____

_____

_____

_____

_____

Write down your thoughts and how you can become your own personal change agent in this area.

_____

_____

_____

_____

_____

_____

Social Capital

As I indicated earlier, my friends often joke with me that I am a master networker. Initially, my interest was not necessarily to help myself. I have been involved in nonprofit management for over 20 years and very early in my career I desired to use the information I obtained to help others. Meanwhile, I noticed information that I gathered and received also benefited me. This information opened doors for me both personally and professionally. Individuals wanted to meet with me to brainstorm. I connected them with others, but I learned that organizations also wanted to obtain this wealth of opportunities which enabled their access to funding, media, or programming prospects with other individuals and organizations.

I had no idea about the concept of social capital. Although networking is a term used interchangeably for social capital, I realized it was much more than this. I discovered that social capital does not mean anything if individuals do not understand how to build relationships. Trust and leadership play critical roles in the development and maintenance of social capital. As a leader in an organization, I could not be effective if I was the only one with the knowledge of how to utilize those resources. I had to create an environment in which social capital and the sharing of information was valued.

Having social capital has assisted me in a number of concrete ways. As a college student, I taught diversity classes to high school students on weekends as a volunteer. This opportunity provided exposure to professionals in higher education. I was completing my degree almost a year later and the director of a local college preparatory center called and offered me a position. If I had not maintained the relationship and been involved in that particular network, I might not have been afforded such an opportunity. She informed me that although the position had to be advertised to a variety of outlets, I could be assured that the position was mine. This was truly an example of social networking that resulted in employment.

My life experiences have brought me to the conclusion that social capital is a necessity, especially for women. The reality of the glass ceiling makes opportunities few and limiting. Recently I was conducting a workshop with a group of women who were from a variety of socio-economic backgrounds. The topic was goal-setting, one that all the women could relate to the discussion. What I noticed is that women of different backgrounds generally are not in the same place to share experiences. One participant wanted to write her memoirs and didn't have the skills to do so. Another participant was a PhD graduate and offered her services.

It was obvious to me that despite differences, there are many commonalities. Forums must be created for women of varying levels of education and experience to connect and share. In doing so, we create a legacy of opening doors for other women who can learn how to develop and/or use their social capital. After more than twenty years as a nonprofit manager, it is my desire to pass on the community-building assets of social capital to other women by helping them learn how to connect their own self-discovery to individual and organizational growth and well-being.

The Distinctions Between Physical, Human and Social Capital

Physical Capital	Human Capital	Social Capital
What you have	What you know	Who you know
Finances	Experience	Relationships
Tangible Assets (e.g., factory, equipment, patents, data)	Education Skills Knowledge Ideas	Network of Contacts Friends

Many in our society focus heavily on education since the attainment of knowledge and experience offer credibility to our resume. Although human capital is necessary in a world that emphasizes the value of a college education, without building strong relationships a college degree could simply become a piece of parchment. It is through the establishment of relationships and networks that one is able to have an opportunity presented because of knowing "the right people." Having financial capital is important but without having a social network that can provide inside information, an investment might prove to be extremely risky.

"It is not what the individuals know but who they know that consistently maintains the gap between men and women's income and position attainment."[7] Women must begin to deliberately develop relationships and networks that are not transactional but transformational. Transactional relationships are about making and closing a deal. Transformational relationships are about authenticity in making sure it is a win-win for those involved.

---

7 Y. Suseno, A. Pinnington, & J. Gardner (2004) "Gender and the Network Structures of Social Capital in Professional-Client Relationships" Advancing Women in Leadership, 24. Retrieved from http://news-business.vlex.com/vid/gender-structures-client-relationships-63914579

The definitions of social capital are numerous but all imply the involvement of individuals and/or networks who invest in a relationship that generally creates some type of benefit in the form of knowledge, association, or financial reward. Depending upon the need, various types of capital are used in our day to day interactions. The challenge is that if individuals do not understand how to build the most basic relationships in order to excel, they are at a disadvantage, especially in a society dependent on human interaction, whether such interaction is face to face or technological. As a result, the need for understanding the impact of social capital is critical in order to have strong business and to accumulate financial, organizational, cultural, and human capital. Social capital allows one to initiate and generate transactions relationally, empowering one to broker for advancement and the growth/well-being of their organization.

The volume of the social capital possessed by a given agent depends on the size of the network of connections he/she can effectively mobilize and on the volume of the capital (economic, cultural, or symbolic) possessed in his own right by each of those to whom he/she is connected.[8] Social capital includes trust, norms, and networks of a social organization, and enables improvements to the efficiency of society by facilitating coordinated actions.[9]

Americans are overwhelmed by their professional and personal responsibilities which have kept many of us from connecting. The challenge America faces is the lack of relationship building which is creating a decline in "civic virtue." Social capital allows individuals to build relationships and

---

8   P. Bourdieu (1986) "The Forms of Capital" Handbook of Theory and Research for the Sociology of Education, Greenwood Press, New York, p. 51.

9   R. Putnam (2000) "Bowling Alone: The Collapse and Revival of American Community" New York, NY: Touchstone, p 19.

access to information and resources, thus keeping people engaged and connected.

All of the women in my initial group expressed disappointment that the group would eventually come to an end. Many felt there were not enough opportunities for women to connect and share. The Wall Street Journal article entitled, "High Power and High Heels" reaffirmed this need. "But a growing chorus is saying that there's nothing wrong with recognizing that women have different tastes and different interests. Besides, after years of being subtly and not-so subtly excluded from male gatherings, women say they want their own space....it's important that women in business and the professions support one another."[10] It is important that we create opportunities for women to connect to one another.

---

10   C. Hymowitz (2007) "High Power and High Heels Companies Move Beyond Sports, Steak and Scotch To Cultivate New Clients" Wall Street Journal. Retrieved from http://online.wsj.com/article_email/ SB117486823975848521-lMyQjAxMDE3NzI0NjgyNjY4Wj.html

Rules of Engagement

The term "Rules of Engagement" is used by military and police forces to describe the circumstances and manner in which force is to be applied to a situation. In other words, the rules establish when and how a battle is to be fought. The rules provide guidelines for making the proper encounter in any given circumstance.

I have chosen to use the term in our discussion of relationship building because the rules that follow provide the proper means of encounter. They will guide us in our engagements with others. In order to build the kind of healthy relationships we all desire, these rules are essential. They are based on the three categories we have already discussed. They have also been accumulated from my observations in working with others and becoming a "master networker" myself.

Rule #1: Identifying your Passion Connects You to Your Purpose

In one of our group sessions, I thought it would be great idea to have each woman write their own personal mission statements. My thought process was that before we start on this journey it was important that each woman have a grasp of their mission. What I found was that many women had a difficult time writing mission statements or setting goals because so much of their identity was tied into what others wanted from them or a lack of time to really cultivate their own needs and desires. I was surprised and shocked by this. So we took time to really work through this because having a mission statement provides you a sense of direction. Taking the time to envision the possibilities gave many of the women the chance to rediscover those dreams that had been covered by the needs of their children, families, jobs, and community roles. This one step greatly enhances the social capital we are preparing to build.

Knowing your purpose first starts with knowing your passion.

Resources such as education, finances, memberships, and the social status of one's family are tangible and can assist in developing the behaviors and possessions of an individual. However, intangible resources that as a society we tend not to focus on as often, which include self esteem and a sense of purpose in life, can also assist in this development.

As a child I seldom saw women who pampered themselves. I remember thinking it was selfish when they did. I saw so many of the women in my life taking care of others that I equated self-care with irresponsibility. Having my daughter has helped me adjust my view. I have realized that if I don't take care of myself, I am not able to care for her but I am also teaching her to continue the same madness.

Loving yourself is gaining an understanding of what you love beyond the involvement of others and their approval. Great relationships begin with a love of self and knowing your purpose. Knowing what inspires you is critical. I like the definition that *The M.A.P. Maker* has for the word "passion."[11] "Passion is the energy that comes from bringing more of YOU into what you do." For me, my passion is something that I enjoy so much that I would do it for free. Sadly, earlier in my professional life I undervalued my skills. Over the years, I've learned how to value myself and my passion. Again, loving yourself is critical because when you are able to do so, you also see the value in yourself and what you bring to the table.

One of my favorite terms is coined by Dr. Laura Roberts whose work is based on the concept of "reflected best self." The reflected best self or RBS is defined as an "...anchor and a beacon, a personal touchstone of who we are and a guide for who we can become. (It)...represents a fusion of the reality of lived experience (who I have been at my best) with the idealized sense of possibility for who one can be(come) when

11   C. Rosengren "The M.A.P. Maker" www.mapmaker.curtrosengren. com/passion

one fully embodies his or her best self. The state of being at one's best involves actively employing strengths to create value, actualize one's potential, and fulfill one's sense of purpose, which generates a constructive experience (emotional, cognitive, or behavioral) for oneself and for others."[12]

It is difficult to bring your best self to work, to your family, and within your community when you are unsure about who you are and where you are headed.

ACTION POINT

When are the times that YOU are most present in your life (meaning that you feel most attentive, involved and complete)? Reflect on the times when the definition of others impacted your view and your passion? What was the result?

_____

_____

_____

Knowing that your personal definitions can truly alter how you view relationships and situations in your life, how do you define success, connection, acceptance, trust, anger, love, support, care, friendship, and guilt?

_____

_____

_____

---

12   Laura Roberts, *op.cit.* p.4.

Think about something that you love to do. It is the thing that you would do for free because it brings you such happiness and inspiration. If it is something that you are already doing, how could you take it to another level?

_____

_____

_____

_____

What are the current opportunities in your life that could allow the chance to explore this possibility and cultivate your love?

_____

_____

_____

_____

What are the obstacles that continue to arise that prevent further exploration? How can you address each of these obstacles?

_____

_____

_____

_____

What are the next steps in making this dream a reality?

_____

_____

_____

_____

_____

We have been doing quite a bit of self-reflection and this might be the time when ask why this is important. The intent is not to make you feel bad about yourself or to evoke any negative memories. The purpose is to help you understand what has shaped your views, values, and your perception of self. Often times, people desire to change how they are perceived so more doors of opportunity are opened to them. Building high quality relationships must be authentic and the process of change must be authentic as well. So, as we continue our journey, take the time to challenge yourself to complete each Action Point. Remember, each principle may not fit your current situation at this moment and that is okay. Determining what is important to tackle will allow you to make a commitment to creating change.

Flow[13]

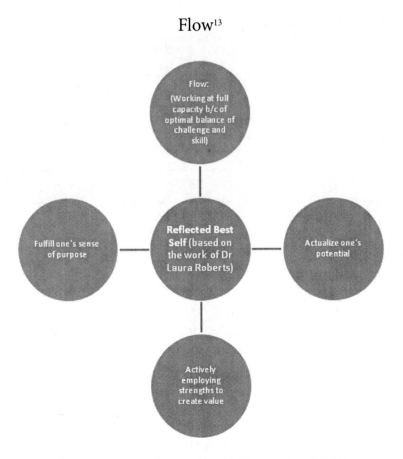

When we are working at our full capacity, fulfilling our purpose and potential, and exercising our strengths, we are engaging components of our best self.

---

13 J. Nakamura & M. Csikszentmihalyi (2002). "The Concept of Flow: Handbook of Positive Psychology" 88-105.

Rule #2: Know Your Purpose to Understanding the Plan

"Where there is no vision, the people perish..." (Proverbs 29:18 AKJV). You are never too young or too old to dream. It doesn't matter how old you are, you can always have aspirations and desires to move forward.

I don't believe that random accidents occur. I believe that from the beginning we were designed to accomplish a task and we are here for a reason. I love the following scripture: "I alone know the plans I have for you, plans to bring you prosperity and not disaster, plans to bring about the future you hope for" (Jeremiah 29:11). This gives me hope and confidence in knowing that in a world often filled with chaos and challenges created by men (and women) that God, from the beginning, designed a special place and role for me.

Life isn't perfect and everything doesn't turn out the way we plan. But it is gaining an understanding that no matter the number of setbacks or the amount of times we mess up, we have the ability to make things happen. When we don't shine and fulfill our purpose, not only does it impact us but others are also affected. Our destinies are tied to one another and if you don't shine, you are losing out on something that could make you a better person.

Over the Christmas holidays, I was fortunate to spend time with a relative who has faced a number of setbacks and has been side-tracked. My cousin, Steven, is in his late twenties. With limited educational and employment opportunities, he feels stuck. He's made some not so wise choices that have made his life more challenging. At one time, he was robbed at gun point. This terrible situation not only traumatized him but has made him fearful. He has defaulted on a student loan but really wants to go back to school. He feels hopeless and doesn't know where to turn.

Are there areas in your life that could create challenges for your dream? Are there things that you have done that might "choke the life" out of your future? Sometimes, we might not have areas of concern and we could do more but made a choice not to do anything. Think about the times in your life that you could have applied more energy, work, time, to a situation and chose not to do something different.

Like most of us when we are overwhelmed, it is hard to see possibilities. Yet, he was open to any opportunity that could change his condition. First, my cousin had to realize that despite all of these awful occurrences, he was still alive. In my mind, that means that there is still something that he has to accomplish on the planet. He isn't finished. Next, we have to take responsibility for what we have done or not done.

In my own life I haven't always made the best choices and I have had to deal with the consequences of those decisions. As a parent, I feel I am responsible for teaching my daughter about life choices. "Plan carefully what you do, and whatever you do will turn out right" (Proverbs 4:26). The decisions we make today can impact our tomorrow. Think about decisions you are making today....could those decisions impact your future positively or negatively? How can these decisions impact your purpose and the plan for your future? We might not be able to reverse those decisions but we can become more aware of our choices, why we chose to do the things we do and the impact of those decisions.

ACTION POINT

I love Laurie Beth Jones and reference her work in most of what I do. In her book, *The Path*, Jones reminds the reader about the mission of Christ and that all of his actions were a reflection of his mission statement. What is your mission statement? Is everything you do a compliment to your mission?

_____

_____

_____

_____

_____

Ten years from now, *O* (Oprah's Magazine) wants to interview you about the impact you've made. What would be the article's focus? Elaborate on what your life looks like in these areas:

- Family
- Financial
- Mental/Emotional Health
- Professional/Education
- Spiritual

Rule #3: Having Goals Is Only Part of the Plan

This is a great place to stop and review what we have discussed thus far. I want to impress upon you the importance of understanding the root influences in your life that shape how you view yourself and the relationships in your life. This is your foundation of understanding why you are who you are today. We then journeyed to understanding why it is crucial to know what our purpose is and how that ties into relationship building.

Now we enter the world of planning and strategy. I was talking to a friend earlier discussing New Year's Resolutions. His comment was "No one ever completes what they start." We all start off with great intentions but somewhere in late February, we miss the mark and find ourselves resorting back to old habits. We often don't take into account the life challenges we face and how that will impact our plan. We can also be our own worst enemy.

This is a great place to park for a minute. One key engagement principle is that we need to scrutinize our attitude about how to build a network and whether you consider relationship building a chore or a choice. If it is a chore, then you will approach each event, and every opportunity as something you dread. It goes back to the saying, "what you think about is what you attract." If you are feeling this way, then an attitude correction is a necessity if you want to surround yourself with the people who can enhance your life. If you are only attending events to build your network, the focus has to change. The goal is to create win-win opportunities for you and for those that you encounter.

My goal last year was to join *Curves* so I could lose weight. About late January (not even three weeks in!), I got sidetracked. I didn't take into account the challenges of starting a new role in my company along with adjusting my schedule to include both work and school. Once I got off track I found it was harder to get back on track.

In our quest for success, we fail to take into account all the external factors that could impact our plans. We often focus on the strengths of the plan never recognizing the possible threats and weaknesses that might be present along the way. As leaders in our homes or in our professional life, we must have a Systems Thinking approach to what we do. Although this view is primarily used in organizational development, we must understand how things influence one another and impact the whole. We often view our challenges by dealing with the specific problem and not attempting to address the overall system that could potentially impact our future.

As a systems thinker, it important to be aware of the following:[14]

Interdependence—Everything is connected. Nothing or no one is independent. All of our actions in some way have an effect on what we do and on our future.

Goal Seeking—We have to know where we are going. What's the point if we aren't seeking some type of result?

---

14 Lars Skyttner (2006), "General Systems Theory: Problems, Perspective, Practice" World Scientific Publishing Company, p.54.

How are your decisions creating the results you would like to see in your life?

Inputs and Outputs—What is it that you need to reach your goal? Quite often, our goals are not consistent with the expertise, guidance, and assistance of others we know.

Entropy—What is the chaos or disorder already present? In all of our lives, there is something present or arm's length away that could create a hot mess.

Regulation—In Systems Thinking for organizations, this generally means feedback. What is the method for feedback for reaching your goals? Are you revisiting your goals periodically or are their others who can hold you accountable and help?

Equifanility means different ways of reaching the same goal. Is there another way that you could reach your goal? It is important to think about alternatives...good, bad, and ugly. I always tell young women to think about the "non-negotiables" in your life. I love the Hall and Oates song, *I Can't Go For That*. In order to know what you want, you have to determine what you don't want and what paths you are not willing to take before beginning the course. Have you identified those?

ACTION POINT

Based on the answer to the *O Magazine* article in the previous question, let's begin to set your goals accordingly. Since that is the long term goal, what will you need to do to make it happen?

_____

_____

_____

_____

What will you need to accomplish in the next 5-7 years?

_____

Next three years?

_____

Next year?

_____

In six months?

_____

_____

Writing the vision down is essential. "Write a vision and make it plain upon a tablet so that a runner can read it" (Habakkuk 2:2 CEB). When most people read this, they only focus on writing down their dreams and goals. It is important to write it so it is clear to you and others. Goals generally serve as inspiration to create movement and can create accountability for you and with others in your life to help you monitor your progress.

In the space below, write your vision for your life. There is a difference in mission and vision. Mission to me is about the here and now. Vision is the end result—what will be transformed as a result of your mission (purpose) being accomplished.

As I mentioned, creating a goal is only half the plan. What cripples most people is that they create plans, have great intentions, but the follow through is where they miss the mark. Think about how many times you said you were going to call that contact for a potential deal. What about the time you sat down, wrote out your entire professional and personal goals, placed them in a location that could be viewed easily, but then forgot to even review them. While many of us are aware of how to create specific, measurable, action oriented, and timely goals, the step we miss is accountability.

ACTION POINT

Select two or three people who can serve as accountability partners in:
- Fulfilling your networking goals
- Completing health/exercise goals you have
- Reconnecting to old and new contacts
- Write down who you chose and why

_____

_____

_____

_____

_____

Rule #4: Knowing Who You Are Is Important

I realized early on that the value and impact of relationships was directly related to how my past was impacting my future. It became a self-fulfilling prophecy until I realized the importance of validating self. So often, we create facades in our personal and professional relationships, which are rooted in our past, with fears that someone will see just how flawed we are. Often in our professional life we strive to appear as though we have it all together, we are at the top of our game, and sadly that is not always the case. The same goes for our personal life. We pretend to be someone we are not, to be more accomplished or skilled than we are, and we attract those in our lives who are a product of the reflection we've provided to the world. We then wonder why many of our relationships are unfulfilling.

I recall a young lady who was brilliant, smart, witty, and very creative. I wanted to have her join my team because I knew she would be a great asset. Her resume read very well and her past experiences were varied and showed her depth of skill. Before bringing her onto our team I contacted all of her listed references who equally shared how talented she was as a professional. After my best effort to cover all bases, I hired her to join our team.

After a short period of time, I realized that who she presented herself to be was not who she was in the workplace. She was still creative; however she was not skilled in the areas she promoted during her interview. I was rather disappointed and her unwillingness to learn and be coached cost her the job. I learned a valuable lesson in this situation. Many of us go through the day wearing a mask that covers up who we are. We are afraid of exposure not recognizing that our limitations can make us limitless when we understand them and know our boundaries. This young lady not only hurt the organization but she also damaged her credibility and an opportunity to grow.

It is when we are authentic about who we are and our needs that the lens that clouded our view begins to change. We will experience growth and invite those into our world when we reflect who we truly are. When my lens changed, I became fascinated with building high quality connections that were mutually beneficial and supportive.

That change occurred while attending a workshop that made me realize God's love for me. I was so upset with God because I had prayed that my dad would be healed from cancer. I really believed that God was going to make my father well through the chemo treatments and other prescribed treatments. Nothing worked. I was so angry with God because I felt my prayer was not answered. For years, I didn't realize that my anger was blocking me from having the relationship I needed with God. I had to not only forgive myself for several past decisions but also I realized that it was time to deal with my unforgiveness toward others including God. I strongly believe that even in my pain, God was there, hurting with me and wanting more for me. God is with us at all times and wants to be a part of our lives.

We are all a part of something greater than ourselves. Knowing how you are connected to God helps you to see yourself in a very different light. If you see yourself as a part of a loving Creator who from the beginning had a design for your life and for the lives of others, you are not only more aware of your purpose but also willing to recognize the possibilities that exist in others.

ACTION POINT

Are there times when you have not been authentic or honest in a relationship? What has been the result?

_____

_____

_____

_____

Is there something blocking your spiritual growth and formation?

_____

_____

_____

_____

_____

_____

_____

_____

Is there an area of unforgiveness in your life? With yourself? With someone else? With God?

_____

_____

_____

_____

_____

_____

How do you think God sees you? Feels about you?

_____

_____

_____

_____

What can be done differently to make your spiritual walk more meaningful?

_____

_____

_____

_____

_____

Rule #5: What You See Is What You Get

At the first session of the women's group, I asked the participants to introduce themselves. It was interesting because, as I expected, everyone talked about what they did professionally. For most women, we define ourselves by what we do for a living and not who we are.

The purpose of the group was to see if women would share their relationships with one another but instead, they shared themselves through their life stories. As women, I believe our emotions and experiences play a role in the way we live in the world. The women of the group demonstrated that we trust one another based on our psychological connections with one another. We are willing to share our relationships with one another when we are able to truly know a person and identify with them.

Networking cannot be only about receiving a business card. It is sharing a story. It is important to know who people are and have an understanding of their journey in order to see where you can go together. I love the Chinese proverb, "If we don't change direction, we might end up where we're headed!" If you don't know who you are and where you are going, it will be difficult to have an understanding of how to connect with others on a deeper level.

One of the most eye opening moments for me was a book entitled, *Reframing Organizations: Artistry, Choice and Leadership.*[15] The book revealed how leaders must apply a different lens to a situation just as an eye doc-

> *The lens you apply is important and will determine the outcome. Are you using the appropriate lens as you deal with life's lessons?*

tor must do so to determine the sight challenges of the patient. Authors Bolman and Deal, share four frames that can identify the problems that exist in organizations (structural, human resources, symbolic, and political). I think the same perspective should apply with individuals and how we deal with our lives.

ACTION POINT

As you evaluate your life, what lens would you apply? Is it a life full of strengths despite the setbacks or a life that has more problems than possibilities? As you examine relationships, consider the following:

Take into account the stories of those involved. What is it that everyone wants to achieve? Can the differences that exist be resolved?

_____

_____

_____

---

15 L.G. Bolman & T.E. Deal, (2011). "Reframing Organizations: Artistry, Choice and Leadership." Jossey-Bass.

_____

_____

_____

_____

Is it possible that the lens required might need a relationship view—are there human needs and emotions to be considered?

_____

_____

_____

_____

_____

Could it be that the challenges have a historical context that has not been taken into account—possible stories, cultures that you could be unaware of?

_____

_____

_____

_____

_____

_____

Are there other extenuating factors such as power struggles and conflicts at work? Evaluate a current situation that is going on in your life. Using the previous questions, how could your perspective change regarding your stance? After answering the questions, do you have a different view?

_____

_____

_____

_____

_____

_____

_____

Rule #6: Your Gratitude Fuels Your Attitude

My daughter says that hope is something that pushes you to do more. Our world is filled with hopelessness. Many people do not have the resources they need to get out of conditions of poverty and injustice. Hopelessness is akin to feeling trapped. When I viewed the video footage of the New Orleans residents after Katrina, I saw hopelessness and feelings of abandonment. It was the love and support of others who offered a shoulder to those in pain. Many of us will experience moments in our life that we feel defeated. In those moments, it can be difficult to see a way out.

In the first group session, the women talked extensively about the challenges they faced in their lives. One of the women expressed the pain she endured through an abusive marriage with a husband addicted to drugs. She left the Midwest and moved with her four children who were school-aged at the time to find a better life for her family. In doing so, she gained the strength to believe she could do anything. Her perseverance, faith, and support system of friends gave her the courage to move on. Her children are now adults. She owns her home, has a car, and recently graduated from college.

Another group member revealed her mother's addiction to drugs and incarceration. Not having her mother at her college graduation made a significant impact on her life. She decided that this loss in her life was something that would be used as fuel to help move her career forward but also to impact the lives of other young women through the creation of a nonprofit organization devoted to girls with mothers in prison. In addition to becoming a CPA, she passed the Bar exam and is now an attorney at a prominent firm. She accomplished

> *Life presents us with challenges. Are you dealing with life or is life dealing with you?*

all of this in her late twenties. Her moments of pain were used to make a difference in her life and the lives of many young girls.

There were many stories of determination and the ability to overcome. I noticed that for each of the women who shared, they all had the belief that they were valuable and deserved a better life. Their experiences served as a foundation for their future and that they knew that somehow, someway, it was possible if they only believed and had hope.

The poem by Emily Dickinson, *Hope is the Thing with Feathers,* exemplifies that in these moments, hope must be something we hold tight:

"Hope" is the thing with feathers
That perches in the soul
And sings the tune without the words
And never stops at all.

And sweetest in the gale is heard;
And sore must be the storm
That could abash the little bird
That kept so many warm.

I've heard it in the chilliest land
And on the strangest sea,
Yet, never, in extremity,
It asked a crumb of me.

I love this poem because, despite the storm and the adversity the bird faces, it continues to sing. Hope flies and lives within and when we face those difficult situations, it is hope that keeps us comforted.

It is interesting that the Bible in 1 Corinthians 13 reminds us that faith, hope, and love are all important. Love is connected to hope. When we love ourselves and see our possibilities, we are activating our willpower and way power. When we are able to believe what God says about us and recognize who we are, we are then able to use those elements to fuel our faith and hope in ourselves and our future.

ACTION POINT

Think back to a time when you felt hopeless. What happened, what was the outcome?

_____

_____

_____

_____

_____

_____

How were you able to make it and presevere?

_____

_____

_____

_____

What lessons have you learned that can help you address your current challenge?

_____

_____

_____

_____

For the next week, begin a gratitude journal. List three things each day you are grateful for even if things are not the way you'd like them to be at this time.

> *Having a spirit of gratitude can truly help you with your attitude to keep you sane in those times of pain.*

Rule #7: Bouncing Back is a Choice

When I was fifteen, I remember being sick at school. My parents sent my grandfather to pick me up. I begged to go home but instead he took me to his house that he shared with my grandmother for over 40 years. Granny was at work and I immediately climbed into her bed. Soon after, the phone rang. A neighbor around the corner from my house called to let us know that my home was on fire.

The fire started in my room. I lost clothing, records, teddy bears—a lot of items that were significant in the life of a teen girl. I remember returning to school the next day with my clothes reeking of smoke. As much as I tried to pay attention, I couldn't because so much of my existence went up in flames. My family decided to stay with different relatives. My brother and I moved in with our grandparents while my parents lived with my mother's brother and his wife. For the first time in my life, I experienced the feeling of displacement. I couldn't see what the future held for me and my family. I just knew that at that moment, I didn't know what was next.

I eventually moved to my aunt and uncle's home with my parents so I could ride with my friends to school. Much of that time was a blur. I lost my hair due to the stress and I struggled with my skin. At a time when I already felt awkward, this experience made me feel even more insecure.

As I look back and think about that time, I can't provide a list of wonderful tips on how to get over pain. I know that my faith in God at a young age was present and even though I felt it wasn't fair, I just believed God was with me. More than 25 years later, I am still here...I can talk about getting through that saga and many others in my life. I still feel the pain and it is a testimony that I am able to share with others. I made it!

In order to deal with emotional hardships, we have to make a choice whether we will sink or swim. There is always darkness before the dawn. One thing is certain—change is inevitable. Yet, the decisions we make will impact the type of change we will experience.

I had a client, Kelly, who was offered an amazing job opportunity. She had been laid off for about three years and had just exhausted her 401K and life savings. She was a wife and mother to four little boys. Being laid off from a company where she spent 19 years caused a major upset in the balance of her family and their finances. So when she received her job opportunity it was like manna from heaven.

She and her family had to uproot from Seattle to Atlanta in a matter of two weeks. As with all major moves, she moved her family across the world to a place none of them had been before. While excited about the new possibilities they would have, they were equally scared about all the unknowns. As they were getting situated in their new home, new church, and new schools, it appeared as through things finally settled for her family.

However, after a year at her new job, her company announced they were downsizing. Sadly, Kelly was laid off again. This news was a major blow and it took a toll on her family and her marriage. She was placed back in the position of trying to figure out what to do, as well as deal with the reality that her family was again uprooted. The one major difference this time was Kelly's resolve that she was not going to allow this to shatter her life. She had built a great network of contacts from the last time she was laid off and had learned the art of building relationships while in her new position. This proved to help her locate a new employment opportunity.

In your personal and professional life, there will be difficult moments. In the article, *The Hard Side of Change Management*,[16] a concept is used for organizations to determine the success of projects. The article encourages organizations to identify one of three categories to determine effectiveness. The same three categories I believe are important to rate situations in our life and their impact so that we respond accordingly:

"Win" is an area that is equivalent with success
"Worry" is an area of concern but can be adjusted/fixed
"Woe" is destined for mediocrity or failure"

ACTION POINT

As you evaluate your current state, use the following chart to determine where you are in each area.

	Win	Worry	Woe
Financial			
Spiritual			
Mental			
Emotional			
Physical			
Family			
Career			

---

16 Harold L. Sirkin, Perry Keenan, and Alan Jackson. "The Hard Side of Change Management." Harvard business review 83.10 (2005), 108.

For those areas that are in the "worry" category, what can be done to turn those worries into wins?

_____

_____

_____

_____

For those areas that are "woes" can you bounce back and let them go?

_____

_____

_____

_____

_____

Rule #8: Change Isn't Easy - Do It Anyway!

Sometimes we find ourselves in relationships or situations that are not beneficial to our growth. On the professional side this can be in the form of not creating boundaries with your team, your peers, or your clients. Another example can come in the form of retaining clients that hinder your growth rather than propel it. We have all had situations where we knew it was time to end a professional relationship. However, we decided to hang on to the relationship longer than we needed to, thus creating an unhealthy environment for ourselves and ultimately impacting those around us.

In our personal lives, this can be holding onto relationships that are toxic to our dreams and goals. This can also manifest in your family ties and through your sphere of influence. These relationships affect our identity and our ability to build fulfilling enduring relationships. It is rare that you will find someone who doesn't have at least one of these types of relationships in their life. The key is to think about those relationships that are hindering you and then make a decision to change them. Change is difficult and uncomfortable. As creatures of habit, we tend to stay in relationships, not because we like them, but because we are afraid of the unknown.

Often, the change brings up our limiting beliefs. For most people, anything risky or new causes us to open the whole file we keep in our brains about failure, needing to be accepted/loved, being seen/exposed, and more that we are not willing to deal with at the time. The challenge is that we often believe these messages. Unfortunately, this can keep us from trying things that could make us incredibly happy.

The reason that change is an issue with networking and relationship building is that the face of networking changes consistently. I would like to look at one big change to networking and that is social media. Social media has become an integral part of building connections. I will be the first to share with you that I am a firm believer that the best relationships are built face to face; however social media has helped to maintain connections.

Social media allows us to discover, connect, and engage with new people of interest. While most people are open to new connections and receiving messages from people they don't know, there is a fine line between reaching out and "spamming." The challenge is to make a connection clearly and effectively without wasting a person's time. Many of us are on both sides of this relationship—sometimes making the connection, sometimes receiving the invitation. To help navigate these waters, I've decided to share some key differences between social media and social networking. There is always a discussion about understanding these terms.

The differences between social media and social networking are just about as vast as night and day. There are some key differences and knowing what they are can help you gain a better understanding on how to leverage them for your brand and business.

Social media is a way to transmit or share information with a broad audience. Everyone has the opportunity to create and distribute. All you really need is an internet connection and you're off to the races. On the other hand, social networking is an act of engagement. Groups of people with common interests, or like-minds, associate together on social networking sites and build relationships through community.

Social media is more akin to a communication channel. It's a format that delivers a message. Like television, radio, or newspaper, social media isn't a location that you visit. Social media is simply a system that disseminates information to others. While it has great benefits in allowing you to maintain your relationships and get introduced to potential clients, it does not replace the importance of face to face networking. With social networking, communication is two-way. Depending on the topic, subject matter, or atmosphere, people congregate to join others with similar experiences and backgrounds. Conversations are at the core of social networking and through them relationships are developed.

It can be challenging to obtain precise numbers for defining the return on investment (ROI) from social media. How do you put a numeric value on the buzz and excitement of online conversations about your company, service, product, or brand? This doesn't mean that ROI is null, it just means that the tactics used to measure are different. For instance, influence, or the depth of conversation and what the conversations are about, can be used to gauge ROI. The return on investment in social networking is a bit more obvious. If the overall traffic to your website is on the rise and you are diligently increasing your social networking base, you probably could attribute the rise in online visitors to your social efforts. So you can see how social media and social networking can work together.

Social media is hard work and it takes time. You can't automate individual conversations and unless you're a well-known and established brand, building a following doesn't happen overnight. Social media is definitely a marathon and not a sprint. Because social networking is direct communication between you and the people that you choose to connect with, your conversations are richer, more purposeful, and more personal. Your network exponentially grows as you meet and get introduced to others.

Social media and social networking do have some overlap, but they really aren't the same thing. Knowing that they are two separate marketing concepts can make a difference in how you position your business and career going forward.

Change is not the only challenge that we face. Balance is also another area that can create panic and concern. For women, I find that we have a hard time trying make the changes in our lives that will create more balance because that means we have to adjust or give up something. Many of us spend so much time proving that we are capable of doing a job that we often sacrifice our family and personal time.

I remember when I first had my daughter I did not want to be perceived as unable to take on as much work as the men around me. I didn't want to refuse travel opportunities and there were a few times I missed important events in her life because of my own worries about what others thought. Women often have to deal with the issue of change because we have the pressure of needing to consistently prove our worth in professional settings; we struggle to create a sense of normalcy for our children while pursuing our personal interests, all while dealing with feelings of guilt. Am I saying that men don't deal with change? Absolutely not! However, my experiences as a woman allow me to look at how we have to change consistently and I understand the difficulty.

Here are some of the biggest and scariest changes we may deal with in our lives:

- Getting married
- Getting separated and/or divorced
- Moving to a new town, city or country
- Having children
- Starting a new job

- Quitting or losing a job
- Starting a new business
- Letting go of an existing business
- The loss of a loved one
- A major health scare

The most interesting thing I have found in my own life, and from observations of those around me, is that even though a change might seem like a negative or stressful event at the time, with perspective and distance, it turns out that the change can create growth (if we allow it) and that life continues to move on.

ACTION POINT

Think about a situation in which you must make a change whether in your professional life or personal relationships. Then ask yourself the following questions.
What is the risk of not changing?

_____

_____

_____

_____

_____

If I wait long enough, will the change just go away?

_____

_____

_____

What are my choices during the change process?

_____

_____

_____

_____

What are the potential consequences to me if I don't change?

_____

_____

_____

_____

_____

What are some things that need to change in my life but I am unwilling to make the adjustments?

_____

_____

_____

_____

_____

How does this affect my personal and/or professional life?

_____

_____

_____

_____

_____

If I don't address the issue, what will happen?

_____

_____

_____

_____

_____

Your focus on growth and addressing change can impact your life in many positive ways. Your honesty will serve as a light to life and help you address important issues that if unresolved, can become detrimental for your desired outcomes. There are two strategies that are usually at work in our lives: self-focused and other focused. At the basis of the other focused strategies is the idea of transformation. In seeking to better your life, you will create a reflection for those around you to view of the process of positive life changes. This goes back to the adage that it is easier to help someone with things they are processing than to face our own reflection.

However, there is a strong benefit to helping others while you are in the midst of your own personal journey with creating more impactful relationships. You are more open to connecting, to actively listening to what others are saying versus waiting for them to finish talking. You are more engaged and you become more intentional. When we are able to understand others and have a deep sense of commitment to their being and success, it creates a better understanding between all involved. Understanding the point of view of others is critical in establishing mutually beneficial relationships.

Another element of change when forming a relationship whether personal or professional is to make sure you know and respect their world. For example, I had a client who was really interested in speaking to college campuses in her area. She had met a Student Leadership Director who served as the Regional Director for an organization that worked with leadership directors at various colleges. She formed a great relationship with this director and was expecting available doors of opportunity as a result of their connection. She contacted this director several times between July and August. She was very frustrated that she was not getting a call back or having her emails returned. What she didn't take into account was that between July and September was the busiest time for this director. She was preparing the students returning to campus, setting up the leadership camps, hosting several parent weekends and a host of activities. So I had to share with my client that just as important as it is to get to know someone it is equally important to understand their world. It is critical to remember that others have lenses as well in which they use to view their world. Your role is to understand those variables that can impact your relationship.

> *"Women can increase their chances for professional success by developing networks that connect them to key individuals, assignments, and resources within and outside of organizations."*
> (Reimers-Hild, Fritz, and King)

It is interesting to note that in the process of creating intentional change, an individual must have trusting or resonant relationships that enable a person to experience and process the discovery. In essence, in order to change relationships, we must be willing to self-reflect. Do you take the time to reflect? Do you have individuals in your life who you trust and can provide a different perspective to guide you in reaching your goals? Can they see/understand things that you might miss?

ACTION POINT

What are some things that I know I need to change in my life but I'm unwilling to make the adjustments?

_____

_____

_____

_____

_____

How does this affect my personal and/or professional life?

_____

_____

_____

_____

_____

_____

_____

If I don't address the issue, what will happen?

_____

_____

_____

_____

_____

If I choose to address it, what might the outcome be?

_____

_____

_____

_____

_____

_____

Rule #9: Choose to Live Positively

Optimism is identified as a positive outlook but it is not an unchecked process without realistic evaluation. "Hope consists of both will power and determination to achieve their goals and 'waypower' thinking (being able to devise alternative pathways and extenuating plans to achieve a goal in the face of obstacles)."[17] Optimism is a socially valued trait and optimists tend to be well-liked by others and have larger social networks. Optimism brings about positive outcomes in relationships by promoting favorable expectancies, which in turn causes individuals to pursue relationship goals more flexibly and persistently. Individuals who are resilient have the ability to deal with stressors and "are open to new experiences, flexible to changing demands, and show more emotional stability when faced with adversity."[18]

ACTION POINT

Your Lens on Life: Is the glass half empty or half full in your view? Do you find you are more optimistic or cautious about your relationships and decisions? Ask this question to two

---

17   Avey, Luthans, Jensen, *op. cit.*, page 681.

18   *Ibid.*

or three people you trust. What was their response?

_____

_____

_____

_____

_____

_____

A positive outlook has a tremendous impact on the way
we network with others. Being optimistic about our future
allows us to look beyond our current situation and focus on
future opportunities. Others will notice this about us and be
attracted. Earlier I shared about a research group of women
that I assembled to learn more about the rules of engagements. At the first session of the women's group, I asked the
participants to introduce themselves. It was so interesting
because, as I expected, everyone talked about what they did
professionally. Why was that interesting? Rarely do we introduce ourselves by sharing about our interests, favorite things
or anything personal. We jump right into sharing about our
professional life and accomplishments.

For most women, we define ourselves by what we do for
a living and not who we are. However, think about the foundations of your best connections. Was it learning the titles of
what they did or hearing about all their accomplishments? I
would venture to believe it was those times where you shared
what your child did the other day that drove you crazy or
about the co-worker that can't seem to get along with any-

one....basically you talked about the things that impact living and not your accomplishments.

The purpose of the group was to see if women would share their relationships and experiences with one another. Remember this was a very diverse group of women so I was not sure what this research would yield. Surprisingly, they shared themselves through their life stories. As women, I believe our emotions and experiences play a role in the way we live in the world. The women of the group demonstrated that we trust one another based on our psychological connections with one another. We are willing to share our relationships with one another when we truly know who a person is and we can identify with them.

Now I have heard many say that you will rarely walk into a meeting and start sharing about your kids and family. I agree. However, when you go to a meeting, you can start a conversation by listening. My boss says something that I love. Whenever he meets a person, he always restates a person's name and then asks them, "What's your story?" I think we spend so much time talking that we don't take the time to find out what we have in common with another person. It is in those moments of listening that we can develop high quality connections.

Low Quality toxic connections deplete and degrade whereas High Quality Connections or HQCs can deal with the rollercoaster of emotions (good, bad and ugly) that life presents. In the midst of the emotion, either person feels safe to share or listen. Another characteristic of a HQC is the ability to endure changes, conflicts, and tensions in the circumstances. People who are involved in High Quality Connections feel positive, a sense of being valued, and are completely engaged. Research has demonstrated the health benefits of these types of relationships such as lower blood pressure, longer life spans, and the ability to deal with stress.

Conversations may seem easier when two people have something in common, but you may not find common ground instantly. That is ok! As you listen more, the goal is to learn about the individual and appreciate their experience. In the moments of listening, there are often opportunities for connections that can be explored further. Everyone enjoys talking about themselves and their experiences and you can get them to share by asking "what" "where" "how" and "when" questions.

I have had clients share with me that another reason they have had a hard time trying to create rapport with someone they don't know is that they feel awkward, scared, or unsure of what the other person will say. Allow me to provide a suggestion: listen. The goal is not to have an immediate answer. The goal is the exchange that can result in an opportunity to connect. View relationship building as an everyday exchange of ideas, shared experiences, shared interests, an opportunity to form alliances and to create new avenues for you personally and professionally. In doing so, you will gain confidence in approaching each situation as an opportunity to bond to those we are already familiar with and bridge with those who are different but might have many things in common with us.

Sara, Trisha, Julie, and Nicole were all invited to the city's largest industry show for the year. None of them knew each other but they each had a goal to attend more events such as this to enhance their respective careers and businesses. Look at each of the ways they chose to create a presence and see if you can identify with any of them.

Sara was a seasoned business professional with over 25 years of experience in her field. She was recently promoted to Director of Recruitment for her company as they wanted to expand their presence along the eastern seaboard. She registered for the event but she is not sure if she will attend and will decide the day of the event if nothing better comes up.

When she decides to go, she looks at her clock and notices the event started over an hour ago. She grabs a stack of business cards and forgets all of her recruiting materials. In true Sara fashion, she arrives fashionably late, sticks her nametag on, and instead of going to a table to sit down, she heads for the waiter who is serving drinks and grabs a plate of food. With a drink in one hand, and food in the other, she scans the room and then puts down her drink to check her Blackberry. When she is finished, she decides to drop in on a conversation.

Trisha is a new business owner and she is so excited to share her new business with everyone. She ordered postcards, business cards, and informational DVD's to share with any new prospects. She showed up to the event about 45 minutes early. She figured that maybe she could get a jump start on meeting people before everyone arrives. She made it a personal goal to meet as many people in the room that evening as she could and she accomplished her goal. She shared with each person she met what her business is about, passed out all her materials, and collected as many names and emails as she could. The following day after the event she began calling all the contacts she made. She waited for a little over two weeks for someone to call her back and no one returned her calls or emails.

Julie is an accomplished professional who recently decided to start her own consulting firm. She is highly organized, a strong strategic thinker, and generally builds strong relationships with her peers, colleagues, and potential customers. She was very excited about attending this event. She arrived 15 minutes early, was prepared with her business cards and had reviewed the invitation list prior to attending. She contacted a few people she felt would be a great connection prior to the event to begin the process of determining if a possible synergy existed. When she arrived she had her targeted list ready to go. Julie worked the room like a pro.

She talked, mingled, and met a number of people whom she could form strategic relationships with. As she drove away that night she felt very proud of herself, as she felt she met her intended target groups, and walked away with great contacts.

Nicole was similar to Julie. She had a great career and decided to build a consulting business on the side. She heard about this event and decided to go. She was very excited and looking forward to meeting new people. She decided not to take any business cards as she wanted to focus on really getting to know people. When she arrived at the event, she made it a point to visit with each table to introduce herself to every person, making eye contact and deliberately making a point to get to know each person. She found she was having a great time and that people were asking for her information as they wanted to get to know her better. She didn't leave with a great deal of business cards, but she did leave with several key people interested in setting up a time to meet her.

Think about each person that was illustrated and think about which person you want to meet or talk to. Further think about how many of these women your path might have crossed at an event or community function. Did you feel inclined to meet them, did you enjoy their company and more importantly were any of these women individuals that you would want to connect with later?

ACTION POINT

When attending an event that has a lot of potential contacts, create your own personal icebreakers that will serve as your introduction. Think about how can you start a conversation that will yield a connection but in a way that you feel most comfortable.

The key to asking questions that will enlist a good conversation is asking open ended question. Here are some suggestions of potential icebreakers questions:

- Are you originally from this area?
- If not, ask them to elaborate on their journey to the city. If they are from the area, use it as an opportunity to learn more about their experiences in the area.
- What is something that you like to do in your spare time?
- Why did you choose to attend this event?
- What's the best book you've read recently?

Networking is not only about receiving a business card or about what you feel you can get from that person. Think about your best and most impactful professional and business relationships—what was it that connected you to those individuals? Was it learning about their job or their role?

_____

_____

_____

_____

_____

_____

It is important to know who people are and have an understanding of their journey in order to see where you can go together. If you don't know who you are and where you are going, it will be difficult to have an understanding of how to connect with others on a deeper level.

Rule #10: Trust is Everything

It is so annoying to view an advertisement that entices you to believe that what is being advertised is real. After the holidays, there were a number of sales offered by an airline. Because I travel a lot, I am always trying to find a great deal. An airline that will remain nameless stated in an email blast that flights were $59 one way. When I visited the website, I discovered that this was false. The actual flights began at $99 and exceeded more than $500 in some instances. I was angry because I trusted they were being honest in their sales pitch. I wasted time and energy as a result of this farce.

Often, the same thing happens in relationships. Initially, we are presented one thing and it turns out to be something else. Trust was given and lost because of a fallacy. Trust is a vital element for social capital. Relationships are formed through trust. Social capital is based on trust, networks, and shared interests and values. Trust is conceptualized as an important relational asset of social capital. In order for social capital to exist, individuals must trust one another.

As leaders in our homes, jobs or communities, gaining the trust of those we serve is essential. "Trust between a leader and his or her followers' is a cornerstone of transformational leadership.... (Trust) creates a moral foundation for extraordinary, values-based transformational leadership."[19] Trust allows individuals to bond with one another and therefore creates an opportunity for mutual sharing and the ability to work together productively.

Once you have gone through all the steps that I have shared, the one element that will glue your entire relationship is the foundation of trust. We all have an inner voice that lets you know whether a relationship is right either professionally or personally. Trust that voice. Trust your instincts to know whether the investment of time is necessary in that relationship.

It is equally important to understand that trust is not something you are given. If trusting someone is like making an investment in that person, trust is therefore a form of capital. Like any professional or entrepreneur either building your career

> *"Those who reveal secrets have destroyed trust and they will never find a friend themselves."*
> *Sirach 27:16*

or starting a business, as a leader you have the task of raising and using that "trust" capital for the benefit of the organization. Leaders often mistakenly assume that they acquire the capital of trust by virtue of their position and title. You gain the trust of the people you lead not by the fact that you have been appointed managing partner, CEO, or president, but by the fact that each of them individually and in varying degrees is willing to grant it to you.

As I conducted the women's group, I noticed that women began to trust one another when they felt not only connected through the sharing of stories but also when they noticed transparency and authenticity. It was a choice for each wom-

---

19   A.G. Stone & K. Patterson (2005, August). "The History of Leadership Focus." Paper presented at the Servant Leadership Research Roundtable, Virginia Beach, VA.

an around the table to choose to trust each other. Trust requires knowledge and information. No one can trust another person until he or she knows something about that person. When the door of transparency was open, trust walked in.

Outside of just trusting that inner voice you must also work toward building trust within the relationships in your life. Looking at the professional side of your life, trust can take on many forms such as:

- When you are working on a project with your co-workers you have to trust that each person will responsibly take ownership of their portion of the project.
- If you work in an environment that services customers or vendors they have to trust your product or what you advertise.
- When you give your word that you will how up on time, be professional (remove you will be), or tell your peers that you will complete a task, they have to trust you will do as you say.

When we are initially presented one thing and it turns out to be something else, trust is destroyed. Trust can be given and lost because of a fallacy. Trust is a vital element for social capital. Authentic relationships are formed and built through trust.

When I share this element about trust, almost immediately there are people who will share with me their struggle with trust. They don't feel that you can really build trust until after a long period of interaction. That is why the principle of trust is so critical. However, there are some steps that you can take to help build your trust. The first key in seeking to gain the trust of the people you network with, lead, or work alongside with is to let them get to know you in a way that allows them to evaluate your intentions and the impact that you may have on their interests.

The type of understanding about you that your network (new contacts, friends, family, new partnerships, etc) seek is information that will allow them to make calculations about your future actions with respect to their interests. What this means is that they are not just seeking to learn about your business or what your past was about, but about your capabilities, intentions, and values as they may affect them. One of the important ways you can convey these factors is not just through your own assertions that you are trustworthy but it is as equally important to take the time to get to know the people you intend to form a relationship with.

As leaders in our homes, jobs, or communities gaining the trust of those we serve is essential. Trust between a leader and his or her followers is a cornerstone of transformational leadership. It creates a moral foundation for extraordinary, values-based transformational leadership. Trust allows individuals to bond with one another and therefore creates an opportunity for mutual sharing and the ability to work together productively.

ACTION POINT

When discussing the issue of trust it is easier for us to decide if we want to trust someone or not, rather than looking at whether we are trustworthy. Take some time and assess whether you are someone who can be trusted in your professional and personal settings. Are you trustworthy as a friend?

As a parent?

_____

_____

As an employee?

_____

_____

As a supervisor?

_____

_____

As a leader in your organization or community?

_____

_____

How could you improve and build stronger relationships?

_____

_____

_____

_____

_____

Rule #11: Step Outside Of Your Comfort Zone

In the group, there were a number of dynamics in existence. Several of the women were Christian, which varied from Charismatic to Liberal as well as Muslim and Jewish. Races were varied and the age range was from late twenties to early fifties. For many of these women, they would have never come in contact with one another. Yet, after sharing their experiences, they realized they had more in common than they realized. Many had dealt with substance abuse or mental health issues within their families. Some had experienced divorce or were in challenging marriages. Many were mothers. No matter their differences, they could still connect and find commonalities in their stories.

For many people, it is easy to stay within our comfort zones and only deal with those who are like us. We miss opportunities daily to connect with someone who can enrich our lives and help us reach our full potential.

There are two types of social capital: Bonding and Bridging.[20] Bonding involves connecting to those who are familiar.

20 J.L. Terrion (2006) "The Development of Social Capital Through a Leadership Training Program" MountainRise: The International Journal for the Scholarship of Teaching and Learning, http://mountainrise.wcu.edu/index.php/MtnRise/article/view/69/47

The connection is through like backgrounds, education levels, and socio-economic status. Everyone desires to belong and feel a sense of purpose. Bonding can occur between individuals but also connects groups.

"Bonding social capital is evident in the close knit relations of friends and families who can be depended on for basic survival in times of stress."[21] Bonding is evident during natural disasters. Whether Hurricane Katrina in New Orleans or Hurricane Sandy on the East Coast, residents bonded together to rebuild. It was not uncommon for individuals who lost everything in the storm to move into the homes of relatives. I had friends who had 20 people living with them in three bedroom homes. Many chose to stay with family members instead of moving in with strangers because of the emotional and financial support of family. Bonding can occur in a constructive or destructive way. The recent revolution in Egypt demonstrated the solidarity of Egyptians who live outside of the country with those who still live there. Gang membership represents a destructive form of bonding through a sense of belonging.

The second critical concept is bridging. Bridging is connecting with those who are different. Bridging is developing relationships outside of the familiar network. Bridging is important because information can be received from this type of relationship that can benefit both the heterogeneous and homogeneous communities. The challenge with bridging occurs when social segregation limits the transfer of information to different networks.

Quite often, in communities of color, people tend to stick together because of the comfort of being with individuals who are from similar backgrounds and who understand the challenges faced by discrimination, racism, and classism.

---

21   A. Mathie & G. Cunningham (2003). "From Clients to Citizens: Asset-Based Community Development as a Strategy For Community-Driven Development. Development in Practice, "13(5), 474-486.

It is also a way to avoid the pain and rejection that sometimes exists from being different. As a result, opportunities for interaction with those who are different is limited if almost non-existent when people segregate themselves.

Social isolation is a rarity but social divisions exist due to religious, political, economic, and cultural differences.[22] Social isolation does not allow for the building of social capital because individuals are not connecting or bridging. People tend to stay with the familiar creating a social identity based on their group or affiliation, which often further marginalizes those who are not in positions of power. Challenges like the economy and political differences in the United States and a media that often distorts the truth, create social divisions and keep individuals from connecting with one another.

In order for equality to be fully realized in society, bridging social capital is essential. "…the full potential of social capital as a community economic engine and as a social and economic equalizer can be realized when bridging social capital links people of different family, ethnic, class, or gender affiliations."[23]

ACTION POINT

Are you leveraging your relationships in the groups that you bond with currently?

_____

_____

_____

---

22 DePrete, McCormick, Gelman, Teitler, and Zheng (2008)

23 Mathie and Cunningham (2002) in referencing Putnam's article *The Dark Side of Social Capital*, page 11.

_____

_____

How could you create opportunities to connect with others
who are different and begin bridging social capital?

_____

_____

_____

_____

_____

Rule #12: Identifying Assets Is a Must

When people ask me to tell who I am, I reply that I am a seeker and a connector. I am very clear on what I can bring to the table. I love knowledge but I also find so much joy in connecting people to their purpose and to resources that can help accomplish their goals. For many women, it is difficult to ask for help because we either are afraid of the response or we aren't sure what to ask. Having clarity about what you offer is essential so that you are able to identify potential partners who can assist in the completion of your goals. The following exercise will help you in identifying your gifts as well as suggesting potential partners for your efforts.[24]

---

24 I am a big fan of the Asset Based Community Development work of Jody Kretzmann and John McKnight. I have used their work to help nonprofits build collaborative relationships but find it helpful for connecting individuals to entities that can be allies in their work both personally and professionally. The content on the next few pages is taken from, *Discovering Community Power: A Guide To Mobilizing Local Assets And Your Organization's Capacity—A Community-Building Workbook* from the Asset-Based Community Development Institute School of Education and Social Policy, Northwestern University.

GIFTS I CAN GIVE

GIFTS OF THE HEAD (Things I know something about and would enjoy talking about with others, e.g., art, history, movies, birds).

_____

_____

_____

_____

GIFTS OF THE HANDS (Things or skills I know how to do and would like to share with others, e.g., carpentry, sports, gardening, cooking).

_____

_____

_____

_____

GIFTS OF THE HEART (Things I care deeply about, e.g., protection of the environment, civic life, children).

_____

_____

_____

The following associations, individuals, and businesses are found in every community. How can connections to these possibilities help build your life, your community and those around you?

A Sample Community Asset Map

Associations
    Animal Care Groups
    Anti Crime Groups
    Block Clubs
    Business Organizations
    Charitable Groups
    Civic Events Groups
    Cultural Groups
    Disability/Special Needs Groups
    Education Groups
    Elderly Groups
    Environmental Groups
    Family Support Groups
    Health Advocacy and Fitness Groups
    Heritage Groups
    Hobby and Collectors Groups
    Men's Groups
    Mentoring Groups
    Mutual Support Groups
    Neighborhood Groups
    Political Organizations
    Recreation Groups
    Religious Groups
    Service Clubs
    Social Groups
    Union Groups
    Veteran's Groups
    Women's Groups
    Youth Groups

Institutions
    Schools
    Universities
    Community Colleges

Police Departments
Hospitals
Libraries
Social Service Agencies
Non Profits
Museums
Fire Departments
Media
Foundations

Local Economy
For-Profit Businesses
Consumer Expenditures
Merchants
Chamber of Commerce
Business Associations
Banks
Credit Unions
Foundations
Institutional - purchasing power and personnel
Barter and Exchange
CDCs
Corporations & branches

Individuals - Gifts, Skills, Capacities, Knowledge, and Traits of...
Youth
Older Adults
Artists
Welfare Recipients
People with Disabilities
Students
Parents
Entrepreneurs
Activists

Veterans

Ex-offenders

ACTION POINT

Are there potential partnerships that can be developed based on the content of the Asset Map? In what way?

_____

_____

_____

_____

_____

Which relationships should be initiated between now and the next three months?

_____

_____

_____

_____

_____

_____

_____

If current relationships exist with entities on the asset map, how can you further leverage those relationships?

_____

_____

_____

_____

_____

_____

Rule #13: Mutually Beneficial Relationships Don't Just Happen

In a mutually beneficial relationship, it is critical for all parties involved to exhibit the following: mutual benefit, mutual influence, mutual expectations, and mutual understanding.[25] In many of our relationships at home or at work, we are unaware of the role these elements can play in creating satisfying and complimentary relationships. We affirm others' identity when we take the time to understand who they are.

This is a good place to stop and ask yourself how often do I take the time to understand someone, who they are, where they come from, and what they need. We actually create a disservice and cheat everyone when we are not true to ourselves. How can you create a mutually beneficial relationship if you are not willing to get to know the other party and risk being more transparent yourself?

There is a lost art that can literally transform any relationship in your life. It will transform how you interact with your spouse or the special person in your life. It can radically

---

25   L.M. Roberts "Reflected Best Self Engagement at Work: Positive Identity, Alignment, and the Pursuit of Vitality and Value Creation, Handbook of Happiness."

change the relationship you have with your children. It can deepen the connection you and your friends have with each other. Further, it can help propel you in your professional career or business.

Constructive and healthy relationships help individuals become more authentic in their communication with others and create a sense of security for an individual to explore their own strengths, weaknesses, and abilities. In affirming relationships, individuals can experience criticism and feedback in a way that is not detrimental because they have a point of reference based on the constructive feedback they have received as well. These experiences provide an opportunity for reflection and self-growth. Mutually beneficial relationships contribute to an individual "enacting their best reflected self, employing their strengths in a way that creates a positive experience for them and a constructive experience for others."[26]

All relationships that are meaningful take time and investment. This doesn't happen overnight. It has to be deliberate, intentional, and open. You must be patient in knowing that although the process might not be immediate, your investment will come back to you. It is not about transactions as we build relationships with others. It is about their transformation as well as our own.

ACTION POINT

While this concept may seem obvious to some, when you stop and think about your relationships think about how many are mutually beneficial? How many are one sided? How many of your relationships do you feel  that you are giving more than you getting back? Take some

---

26   *Ibid.*, page 33.

time and evaluate what is being deposited in your life and subtracted in the relationships that you have.

_____

_____

_____

_____

_____

Rule #14: Generational Differences are Important

"Generational succession is, in sum, a crucial element in our story. However, it has not contributed equally powerfully to all forms of civic and social disengagement. The declines in church attendance, voting, political interest, campaign activities, associational membership and social trust are attributable almost entirely to generational succession. In these cases, social change is driven largely by differences from one generation to another, not by changing the habits of individuals. By contrast, the declines in various forms of schmoozing, such as card playing and entertaining at home, are attributable mostly to society-wide changes, as people of all ages and generations tended to shift away from these activities. The declines in club meetings, in dining with family and friends, and in neighboring, bowling, picnicking, visiting with friends, and sending greeting cards are attributable to a complex combination of both society-wide change and generational replacement."[27]

In the last few years, I have taught a number of workshops about generational differences. For the first time in history, there are four generations working and interacting together. There are a number of differences that exist in how

---

27 Putnam, *op. cit.*, p. 265-266.

we interact with one another and as we build relationships it is important to recognize these differences and how characteristics can impact the way we not only view the world but how we connect.

Traditionalists are generally the individuals who are born in the late 1920's to the early 1940's. They are accustomed to formalities and hierarchy. This generation wants respect and values a historical perspective. Baby Boomers are the largest generation to date and were born between the late 1940s and the early 1960s. This is a group that has seen enormous change in their lifetimes such as the Women's Movement, space travel, assassinations of great leaders, and the Civil Rights Movement. In addition, this group is credited for the workaholic trend. They are about change and prefer face to face meetings instead of emails.

Generation X does not boast the numbers of the Baby Boomers. Born in the mid-1960s through the 1980s, this group does not enjoy a lot of meetings and prefers work-life balance. They are a group that researches and resents hypocrisy that they have viewed in previous generations. Lastly, Generation Y or Millenials are the generation that has enormous options. From lattes to MP3 players, this is a group that can see change at the click of a button. They are accustomed to diversity because they grew up with it. This generation does not see the boundaries of age and as a result all adults are the same. If they are an adult, they are equal to another adult regardless of age. Just because you are older doesn't necessarily translate into automatic levels of respect.

I've read so many studies and much of this is a combination of the research and my own observations. I have learned that for many, our ability to connect breaks down when we have to bridge social capital with individuals who are younger. We tend to place our experiences upon them and when those experiences don't line up to what we expected, we are disappointed and begin to find fault.

I was conducting a workshop and I made a dumb comment that I felt young people were apathetic. (If I took the time to remember, people said the same thing about my generation and I wasn't apathetic...I just did things differently.) A young man reminded me that young people today are just as active as previous generations. The revolutions in Egypt and in other parts of the world were conducted by the social media savvy young people who wanted change. He convinced me that the way young people connect might be different than the dinner parties and picnics of the past but there are real interactions that happen daily as a result of Facebook, Twitter, and other social networking sites.

It is imperative that we begin to understand the influences that impact various generations. As I mentioned previously, applying a lens is critical whether it is a structural, political, human relations, or symbolic to a situation. It is also critical to recognize the role of age on how we view the world.

I always tell the story that when I was growing up, there were two types of coffees: Maxwell House and Community Coffee. I remember that important guests at my grandmother's house received Maxwell House although Community Coffee was always served when company was gone. The first time I went into Starbucks I am sure the staff thought I was addicted to crack rocks. I asked so many questions about the differences in a latte, espresso, mochas, and all of their products. To this day, I couldn't tell you the difference in any of them but I know there are a lot more and different coffees now than when I was growing up.

Imagine the impact this has on a young adult. To say that change cannot happen is not in their vocabulary! Older generations feel that no feedback is a good sign whereas I find young people today want feedback and often. Knowing these tips can help strengthen those important relationships and help you create bonds that are long lasting and rewarding. I often share with the young people I mentor that having a mentor is critical. All of us need mentors in our lives especially in the areas where we might need growth. I think it is equally important to obtain friends who are younger and older that can help you with having a sensitivity to these generational differences.

ACTION POINT

Remember when you were growing up; what were some of the things that frustrated older adults about your generation?

_____

_____

_____

_____

_____

How have you changed as a youth to an adult? What are some things that you miss?

_____

_____

_____

_____

_____

_____

If you could offer wisdom to those who are younger, what are three things you wished someone had told you?

_____

_____

_____

_____

Are you mentoring? If so, what could you offer that you aren't sharing? If not, identify a young person at your job or in your community (even an organization) that you could offer your wisdom and insight to.

_____

_____

_____

_____

Are you being mentored? Identify an individual that can help you reach your goals and make a plan to reach out to them.

_____

_____

_____

_____

Rule #15: Create Clear Boundaries in Relationships

I find I am in amazement at those relationships we put so much effort into that yield betrayal and pain. It is difficult to trust again when you have tried to be good to someone who you feel has let you down. This doesn't only apply to lovers but also in professional relationships. What happens when you are mistreated by someone you wanted to help?

Some years ago, I hired a young woman who was kind, compassionate, and an all-around gem. She needed a job and had some basic skills but her personality was exactly what our organization needed. She experienced several tragedies in her young life and often had setbacks. Her family would torment her, especially her ex-husband whose demands were often unreasonable. As a single mother, she struggled rearing her two young daughters. She began to experience enormous grief, anger, and abandonment issues. In my desire to assist her through the challenges, I and the rest of the team tried to be present and accommodate her. Ultimately, the aggression and the emotional outbursts became disruptive and emotionally draining for everyone.

This situation taught me a valuable aspect in relationship building. As we build relations, we cannot allow ourselves to get enamored with personalities. Ultimately, relationships must be beneficial to both parties and if you are always giving to a point that it drains you, the relationship is toxic and unproductive. When I look back, she was hired for the wrong reasons - her persona. In actuality it cost the team time and efficiency.

Not all relationships are healthy. At some point, we must ask the hard questions about our needs and expectations. I failed to analyze that adequately and instead I brought in someone who was damaging because I was not clear. It is important to be clear about non-negotiables and set expectations at the onset of relationships. What is a business relationship to you? What does that encompass? What do you need for success?

For women, we often confuse our business lives and personal ones. I did not have set boundaries in this relationship and as a result, it created ambiguity because of my lack of definition and clear boundaries.

ACTION POINT

The definition of toxic is causing injury or death. Often, many of the relationships we are involved in hurt us in various ways even causing a spiritual death. Create a list of the damage that toxic relationships have create personally and professionally.

List Toxic Action	The Impact (personal or professional)	How has this impeded your progress?

List Toxic Action	The Impact (personal or professional)	How has this impeded your progress?

For each result, list what you can do differently to reverse the damage of this situation.

_____

_____

_____

_____

_____

_____

Rule #16: Be Present

A good friend of mine is going through a challenging time. He has experienced several losses of relatives and friends in the past few years. I believe God brought us together "for such a time as this" because I experienced a similar situation in my life about seven years ago. Losing my grandmother, father, uncle, aunt, and several cousins was tough! In addition to the pain he has gone through, he is struggling with the decisions by his teen daughter. I listened intently. His pain was enormous and he didn't quite understand why she was choosing the lifestyle that conflicted with her upbringing.

I realized that it was not so much about her decisions as it was about his feelings of inadequacy and failure. As I asked him to reveal what was really there, he began to share how he felt embarrassed and wondered if he had done enough.

So much of our pain in relationships resides in this core place in our spirit we are afraid to touch. It hurts to look deep at the core and remove the Band-Aids that are covering scars that appear to be healed but under the surface are still very wounded. My prayer lately has been to see what is real. I think about the rear view mirrors that state things are "closer than they appear." So often, the underlying issue is closer than we realize.

We must own our pain, our expectations, and disappointments. It feels awful to admit that we play a part. If we continue to attract wrong relationships, the common denominator in each of them is you! We must be honest and experience the pain, which for many of us is holding us back from a bright and blessed reality.

In all of this, I am learning to "be"—to be present. As I write this, I am struggling in my own personal relationships. I find that moving forward isn't easy. In the past, I've always moved forward and pushed through pain, which has gotten things done but at my expense and the expense of others. I am learning to be still, own my pain, and become a reflective learner. I can see where I've made mistakes that contribute to my current situation. I also have to begin to see how my past plays a role in my present.

Being present allows you to stand still and absorb all that is good, bad, and ugly in order to make informed decisions. In a microwave society, we want things done immediately. Life isn't about getting the answer right. If you don't understand the process, if you don't pay attention to the variables in the equation, you'll keep getting results that don't add up. Be still. Hear the small still voice. Reflect on the variables to discover your answer.

ACTION POINT

I remember that I wanted my daughter to hear the birds outside of our window. She couldn't. It took practice to quiet her thoughts to be able to hear. The noise drowns out the silence. Think about what you are se to about your life, your next steps. What is in the way of allowing you to be still to listen for the answer?

Find a quiet space in your home and allocate 10 minutes a day to silence. Use that time to process at either the start or the end of your day your thoughts. Increase that time every week to include an additional five minutes with the goal of ultimately taking 30 minutes or more each day to enjoy the quiet and hear the small voice.

Rule #17: Define What You Will Accept

Hall & Oates said it best, "I can't go for that." Our world is intrigued with self-esteem. Infomercials want us to buy products that will make us feel better about ourselves. If we buy the face lift in a box crème we will look ten years younger. No one tells you that ten years later you might grow a third eye. No worries! Put some make up on it and keep moving. Really? Is that the goal? No matter how much we pay attention to the outside, we have to spend time cultivating who we are and whose we are. We are all spiritual beings with an earthly purpose. Beauty will change and sometimes even fade. What is important is to create opportunities that will attract others to you that you need along your journey.

If you don't take the time to examine and reflect on who you are, you will continue to get the same experiences until you choose to do something different.

Most women never analyze the non-negotiables. What are the unacceptable things that you won't allow in your life? A girlfriend of mine from college was dating a man who grew marijuana. She was often afraid of the police arresting both of them although she didn't smoke. She was aware of his behavior while they dated but didn't think he would continue when they moved in together. She was furious but didn't say anything. Her inability to define what was non-negotiable allowed her to push her boundaries further and further away from what was acceptable for her life.

How many times do we push boundaries because we have not defined our non-negotiables or who we are? At some point, for you to connect with others, you must know what you won't accept personally and professionally.

ACTION POINT

Use the template of the mind map below to create your own. In the center, write non-negotiables. List in the connecting circles those things in your life that you cannot accept or tolerate in your relationships both personal and professional.

Rule #18: Save a Lot by Listening

I frequently watch the television show Shark Tank and I must confess – I love Damon and Mark Cuban. I also find it interesting that I must say his whole name – Mark Cuban – when I discuss him. Nevertheless, this show often bugs me. The premise of the show is that entrepreneurs pitch a business idea to a group of investors. Often, these poor entrepreneurs pitch themselves and their ideas without carefully considering the ramifications of their decisions. Even when the Sharks give advice, there is always the unprepared, pitiful one who has to keep selling or arguing his point. Hello! They are the experts–please listen!

One episode was especially intriguing. Billy Blanks Jr. presented his fitness regimen to find funding for a certification program. His DVDs were being distributed through some major outlets. He was asked to consider bundling his retail business with the certification program and allow his program to be distributed by a larger fitness company.

He almost lost a deal that would have allowed him access to millions of consumers, funding from Mark Cuban (see, I did it again) and Damon, and then technical expertise because he was unable to listen. He was so fixated on his brand and all his hard work that it almost slipped through his hands. Damon actually ran after him to re-explain the deal after Billy Blanks Jr. turned it down.

Second chances are few and far between. How often have we turned down opportunities because we focused on the appearance of the messenger rather than the message itself? How often are we so caught up in selling our product the way we envision it being sold without really being open to other possibilities? He almost lost his chance because he didn't listen.

What signs are presenting themselves that you are not listening to? If you listen, what could happen? If you don't listen, what could happen?

ACTION POINT

I remember recently hearing Bishop T.D. Jakes share a sermon about missing opportunities. Often we run from obstacles when they are actually disguised opportunities. What opportunities are presenting themselves that you are not listening to or running away from?

_____

_____

_____

_____

_____

_____

_____

If you listen or turn toward the obstacle, what could happen?

_____

_____

_____

_____

_____

If you don't listen or continue running away, what could happen? What could you miss?

_____

_____

_____

_____

_____

Rule #19: Don't Assume That Common Sense Is Common

In establishing relationships, we often make numerous assumptions about people. We assume they have specific experiences, upbringings, and understanding. As our world becomes more global, we fail to realize that not everyone sees things the same way we do. It is even more apparent in generational differences. There are certain things I won't do. A *Girls Gone Wild* video is not in my future. The idea of allowing others to witness gravity at work isn't my idea of fun. You probably won't see me posting vulgarities on Facebook either, although I am often tempted to write my real unadulterated thoughts on some of the bizarre posts I read. Instead, I am aware of the repercussions of those actions. Many are not. I have several relatives who use Facebook as a venue to share very personal thoughts. No matter how many times they are told anyone can read their comments, they just think I'm being old.

A Human Resources Director of a large company told me they mine through Facebook and other social media to discover information about potential employees. Although we believe the illusions that privacy settings protect us, they don't. Be aware of the personal brand you are creating because it will impact your professional reach.

Do not assume that everyone sees the world like you do. Instead of making assumptions, learn the story behind the person. Be aware that tools like social media are helpful but a means to an end. They can never take the place of true intimacy and face to face connections.

In the book, *Reframing Organizations: Artistry, Choice and Leadership*, the authors discuss different frames or perspectives. I equate this to visiting my doctor to check my vision. Each click drops a new lens for me to view. Sometimes I see clearly and other times, my vision is blurry. The same thing applies in our relationships. They offer four frames that happen in organizations and I believe they also exist in our daily interactions:

- Structural: the rules, regulations, structures that are in place
- Human Relations: the interpersonal dynamics in relationships
- Symbolic: culture and history
- Political: power

My daughter recently posted on Instagram that she was devastated that one of her favorite celebrity couples broke up. Another person posted, "I'd love to have your first world problems." My daughter was offended. I explained to her that she had to see through the lens of this person. Is it possible that she lives in a country that does not allow for much freedom of speech or celebrity watching? Could it be that she is from a different culture that does not view this as important? My daughter only saw it as a personal attack and felt powerless which is how many of us feel, or our emotions catch us and we are angry or embarrassed. In order to be effective in our relationships, we must examine not only our lens but the lens of others.

ACTION POINT

Think of two situations—one professional and one personal—when you applied a not-so-useful lens to view it. Using all of the frames offered, revisit the situation and apply each lens to the challenge in the space be

Professional Situation:

    Structural:

    Symbolic:

    Human Relations:

    Political:

Personal Situation:

    Structural:

    Symbolic:

    Human Relations:

    Political:

Rule #20: Authenticity + Awareness = Start of Something Serious

As I wrote this book, I struggled with my voice. It's always been an area of conflict for me. When I write a paper for school, my professors always ask me, "What do you think?" For some strange reason, I've felt the academic folks were the experts and regurgitating their perspective was more interesting than my own. My professors ask for my insight and reflection, which for me is new. I questioned and doubted if my thoughts were relevant.

In hiding behind the words of some great thinker I was not vulnerable or exposed! I couldn't be told I was wrong because it wasn't my idea to begin with. In doing this, I was playing it safe. I became a writer who said what everybody else said and expressed what I thought my audience wanted to hear. I cheated myself because the very feelings that defined me were locked inside, hidden because I didn't believe it was worthwhile to share or that I would be heard.

For women, many of us have been silenced in our own relationships and as a result, we learn to wear a mask. Some of our masks are designed to protect our pain. Other masks are worn to keep people from hurting us again so we become the assailant. How often do we allow others to influence our voices to a point that it ultimately changes who we are?

As I write this book, I became confused. In my quest to sound like an expert, I listened to so many voices that I became lost in the process. I finally had to listen to what I felt was necessary.

Being authentic is being your true self – good, bad, and ugly. It's being vulnerable and open to all of who you are. It will be difficult to build lasting relationships when you hide from yourself. Knowing those things that trigger your emotions allows you to be open to all of you. If we are so bent on being what others want, we wake up one day pulled in so many directions unsure of who we are and where we are going.

The downside of this behavior is that we begin to attract others who resemble what we have displayed to the world. I meet so many women who are frustrated because their relationships are futile. At some point, we must begin to question what message we are sending to others. If we continue to get superficial friends, what values do we display as important in our lives? Reflection is imperative in the process of authentic relationship status with ourselves.

Michael Jackson's *Man in the Mirror* is a testament to the role of self-reflection to make change. What does your mirror say about you? Are you receiving what you want? Are you expressing the real you or is the face that you show only revealing a piece of you?

Become aware of who you are to create the real relationships that lead to fulfillment and authenticity.

ACTION POINT

In the movie, Shrek, there was a talking mirror. Although this mirror was motivated by fear, it often wanted to share the truth but wasn't able to. If your mirror could talk, what would it say about you?

_____

_____

_____

_____

_____

Are you receiving what you want from life? If not, why?

_____

_____

_____

_____

_____

Are you expressing the real you and if not, what components of you need to be revealed?

_____

_____

_____

_____

_____

Could this lack of full disclosure keep you from achieving what you want?

_____

_____

_____

_____

If you reveal it, what could happen?

_____

_____

_____

_____

If you don't reveal it, what might happen?

_____

_____

_____

_____

Rule #21: S.L.I.P.

One of the most interesting things to me is my inability to lose weight. Well, let me stop lying. I am a serious "carbo-tarian" – I love breads and pastas. I love fried battered food. As much as I love it, you would think it was a reciprocal relationship but it's not. Too much fried food actually makes me sick. Yet, despite the side effects, every so often I crave fried okra, toasted garlic bread, or even milk knowing I'm lactose intolerant.

I know better and yet I will do those things that are not only bad for me but can be detrimental to my health. It's funny how I can recite herbal remedies and even know what I should do but I don't. I want what I want and truthfully, I'm setting myself up for dire consequences. Those consequences have frightened me and now I'm implementing things to make drastic changes.

One of the consequences has been watching relatives age. As a kid, these women were amazing to me. They partied, danced, dressed fabulously, and always seemed to live life fully. I am now looking at thirty years later of that lifestyle. I've lost an aunt to out of control diabetes. She knew better and chose to eat sugar in large quantities. Even when she lost toes, she continued on a path to self-destruction. She missed the birth of her first grandchild. She never saw sixty but had a body that was worn out when she left because of her abuse.

The list goes on and on of women whose choices cost them. In addition to food, there were choices of bad men who abused their minds, emotions, and self-esteem. They were not protected by the very ones who supposedly loved them. Future relationships were jeopardized because they were suspicious and could not trust.

As we look at building relationships, we must analyze our choices and determine how long they could impact our futures. Taking care of others is often a part of the make-up of women. It is the choice that becomes a self-sacrifice which does not rebuild but destroys our very essence that must be evaluated. That's when you...

- **Stop** and take time to pause.
- **Listen** to your instincts.
- **Investigate** by examining past situations and present predicaments.
- **Position** yourself to make the most effective choice based on your data.

When the choice has a short term pay off but a long term penalty, we must count the cost, especially if it creates a lack of balance in who we are. I can eat fries but not every day. Chocolate cake is good but not once a week. I've chosen to exercise on my elliptical which was previously my glorified clothes hanger. I realize that I sleep better when I exercise the junk in my trunk. I am going back to the shakes that allowed me to lose weight before. I know I need a goal and having structure helps me.

Being aware of those triggers in our lives is the beginning of authenticity in ourselves. It is when I'm honest, I'm able to make informed decisions and create beneficial possibilities.

Analyze the people who you attract. Are they helpful or harmful? What is it in those that are harmful that you feel you need? Why is that need important? What do you feel is missing in you that they offer?

ACTION POINT

Think of two situations that involve choices that can impact future relationships. Apply the SLIP Principle.

Stop – What is the best way for you to reverse the decision?

_____

_____

_____

_____

_____

Listen – What does your heart say about it? What does your head say? Are they similar conclusions and if not, what is the tension between the two?

_____

_____

_____

_____

_____

Investigate – How have you dealt with this before? How would you like to deal with it? If you do what your heart says, what is the consequence? If you do what your head says, what is the consequence?

_____

_____

_____

_____

Position – What are the alternatives to your decision? What are the consequences of each? What is the short term outcome? The long term outcome? Based on the data, what is the best decision for you?

_____

_____

_____

_____

_____

Rule #22: Give Permission

This was one of my best birthdays. I was afraid in my twenties to reach my thirties. I really thought I'd have all the answers. My thirties were challenging–I was a new mother and still realizing how much I did not know. I believed when I got in my forties, life would be a breeze. Those self-esteem issues that plagued me for the past twenty years would magically disappear.

I discovered I had been told a lie. I thought everything would come together and make sense. What I soon discovered was that I had become surrounded by magical women who turned on for the public but behind closed doors were miserable. They were incredible illusionists to each other but because they knew the truth, they could not convince themselves of the tricks they pulled daily. There were always the few disillusioned ones but after a glass or two of wine, those houses of so perfectly arranged cards began to tumble.

If we are truly honest, we will admit that we all suffer with insecurities. Our world tells us to lose the baby fat when we have kids never relishing in the fact that we are creators of life. We don't enjoy our pregnancies because we are too busy tearing ourselves down.

I would ask my husband if I looked like a whale or a cow when I was pregnant. Poor guy, he couldn't win for losing.

I would have body slammed him with my hormone levels gone wild at the time if he had said either. I couldn't see my beauty and the ability that God had given us to create a new life because I felt fat.

I always wondered how women kept their houses clean and took care of kids, husbands, and worked in or out of the home. It was to my surprise when I asked a group of successful women how they did it. They were honest. Something went lacking at times–a sink with dishes, dinner was take out —I was forever grateful that the facades were down and we could be real. It freed me and gave me permission not to keep up the illusion of perfection, which I was failing at miserably.

Having "personal summers" are another conversation topic that women run from. I often wondered, when I was in meetings and sweat began to pulsate from my face into dripping beads of water, if others knew what I was experiencing. I would think that maybe they thought I was having withdrawals from crack sprinkles or if I was extremely passionate about the topic that it caused me to break out in what James Brown would say "Gone make wet, gone make me sweat…" I wanted to hide in a hot tub and get away from everyone.

It wasn't until other women began to share stories of their saga with pre-menopause that I felt another layer to sisterhood. As they shared their stories I began to see the commonalities and realized that we are not as different as we think. In my women's research group, after the titles disappeared and the stories of pain, potential, and possibilities were shared, connections developed.

The only way true authentic relationships will happen is when we allow ourselves to be vulnerable. We must give permission to ourselves to be human and frail. That is when we begin to see it in others as well. If I am expecting perfection in others, I am setting myself up for a catastrophe and I am not allowing the other person to be real. I'm then disappointed when they let me down because I wasn't honest with myself about my own expectations.

Our relationships fail because we don't give others permission to be themselves and when they do, we are devastated. When we end illusions, we can then enjoy the magic life brings.

ACTION POINT

What are the illusions you create?

_____

_____

_____

_____

_____

What are the expectations you have of yourself? Of your family? Of others?

_____

_____

_____

_____

_____

_____

What are these expectations based on?

_____

_____

_____

_____

_____

Are they real or perceived? Based on what?

_____

_____

_____

_____

_____

How can you give yourself permission to be more authentic in your relationships? How can this help you personally and professionally?

_____

_____

_____

_____

_____

Rule #23: Sharing is More Than Making a Sale

A friend of mine is one of those amazing folks who can get people to open up. He never starts a conversation about himself. He is very careful to make sure that it is less about him and more about the person he is talking to.

I've learned a lot from him. He is a person who is the embodiment of the term "high quality connections." These are relationships that add to you instead of drain you and make you wish you could watch paint dry instead. He is highly relational and yet, is able to experience impactful relationships with many.

I find that his ability to connect is due to his willingness to listen. He's not concerned with trying to close a deal or get his point across in a thirty second elevator speech. He is much more interested in finding commonalities because he knows if that can bring us together, we can then talk about anything else later.

His first line is, "_____ (name of person), tell me your story." People love to talk about themselves and in several minutes of listening, he is able to identify commonalities. He asks questions and is deeply engaged. He realizes that if he is unable to share his story at that time, he will later because the listener is delighted to have someone who is interested and attentive. He is drawing connections to determine how they can work together while listening.

So often we meet people and "tell" them about our needs and wants and don't take the time to know them to determine if the relationship is information sharing, mutually beneficial, or a key stakeholder in our lives. All relationships have a purpose even if it is to teach us to stay away from certain characteristics. There are those whose sole purpose is to share information. You might not talk every day let alone monthly but they can open doors or vice versa.

A mutually beneficial relationship could be someone who not only blesses you professionally with guidance or connections but also impacts your life in a way that helps you personally. You enjoy their company and they feel the same. A key stakeholder is someone that mentors you or collaborates beyond an idea. Their role is an investor in your life.

It is important to make sure that you are also providing those roles to others.

Share your story but always be willing to listen to others. I hate it when I attend events and the person who approaches me is only concerned about how I can help them. I am more apt to work with those who create "win-win" situations for us both. In all relationships be open to changes and how you can invest to make them grow.

ACTION POINT

Who are the information sharing relationships?

_____

_____

_____

_____

_____

How can these be leveraged more?

_____

_____

_____

_____

How can they become win-wins?

_____

_____

_____

_____

Who are the mutually beneficial?

_____

_____

_____

_____

Who are the key stakeholders?

_____

_____

_____

_____

_____

Rule #24: Recognize Life Shapes and Sizes Each of us Differently

I was returning from a trip to visit my mother when I realized that since my father passed away my mother has found her voice again. My father was very domineering and allowed limited room for variance. If he said it was raining Cheerios from the sky, we knew questioning was pointless. Our obedience was evident when we went outside with a bowl of milk. Some people questioned my mother staying with my father until he passed away. They divorced and remarried when I was in my twenties. It wasn't for everyone to understand. She loved him.

In knowing her story, one would realize that she stayed because she grew up without a father and that shaped her significantly. She felt that her mother's financial struggles would have been reduced had her father stepped up. My dad was a provider and my mom did not want to deprive me and my brother of having a father.

There were both positives and negatives in that decision. I had my father but his inability to connect emotionally wounded me, even as an adult. I will always love him. I will always love my mom because she did what she could and what she felt was best for us. I am grateful because I understood the sacrifice due to my awareness of her story.

As we were driving, I mentioned to my husband a post on my Facebook page from a professional friend. She wished that my upcoming year was calm. I was initially perturbed. What made her think I wanted a calm year? I remembered previous conversations that she expressed her opinion about my schedule. Looking back, she wasn't the first person to tell me they couldn't understand how I kept up school, family, and work. Sadly, I've discovered that we place our lens on others to either limit or compare them to ourselves.

If a woman works she is viewed often as being neglectful to her family. It's funny to me that men who work long hours or travel are not assumed to be bad fathers or husbands. If a woman stays home with her children, she is seen as being boring or having no ambition. I've met mothers who work from home and are activists while their kids are in school or even volunteer at their kids' schools. They are project managers just as the women who collect a paycheck.

It is unfair to limit others because you are using your lens to view their world. We don't ask what shapes, influences, supports, or shares in their decisions. I remember hearing Bishop T.D. Jakes of Potter's House make a statement that there were those who wanted his anointing. What they fail to realize is the fact that he lost both of his parents prior to being a young adult and suffered much hardship. They only saw the resulting fruit. They didn't see the process, the tears, the burdens, and experiences that developed his character.

It is important we not only know the story of others but we must become a systems thinker. We have to understand the variables and factors that shape a person. When we see our story clearly, we can apply the type of lens needed to comprehend the journeys of our fellow travelers. Write your story.

ACTION POINT

What influences and factors shaped you?

_____

_____

_____

_____

_____

What are recurring themes that surface?

_____

_____

_____

_____

How do these themes help or harm you?

_____

_____

_____

_____

_____

How can you adjust your lens as necessary when someone is different or chooses a different path than you?

_____

_____

_____

_____

What are the triggers that set you off about others?

_____

_____

_____

_____

Why does this bother you so much?

_____

_____

_____

_____

Should this be something that signals time for a change in you?

_____

_____

_____

_____

Rule #25: Remove Your Blocks

I was meeting with a friend who is building her business. She has felt obstacles with certain populations and can't seem to understand why she can't grow beyond her existing network. As we talked through her challenge, I noticed the block. It wasn't that these populations ignored her; she had made an invisible wall in her thinking that manifested itself in practice.

I mentioned to her a term in yoga called "intention." She didn't realize that she reinforced this belief through her self-imposed thinking. Often, we attract what we don't want because it is our point of focus. In watching influential speaker and author Iyanla Van Zandt recently, she reaffirmed for me that we attract what we focus on or in many cases, what is broken and unresolved.

Years ago I invited a speaker to present a topic for municipal leaders. Arthur was dynamic and inspiring. After asking him why I had never seen him before, he politely said I wasn't ready. I wasn't sure how to take his response. He asked me about my car which was new. "Before you got it, did you notice it on the road?" I replied no. It seemed that prior to the purchase, no one had it and now that I own it, it is everywhere. He reminded me that I could not see my car previously or even him because it wasn't my focus.

On a deeper level, I saw that so often my own blocks in thinking limit me from accepting and receiving positive experiences. I limit love in my life because I'm waiting for the pain. I dismiss business opportunities because I questioned my value. When my friend identified her obstacles, she was able to conquer the walls that kept her from achieving success. It is only when you face your fears that you can realize your fierceness!

ACTION POINT

What are 3 blocks in your thinking that limit your dreams?

_____

_____

_____

_____

_____

Where did these blocks come from? Do you see patterns?

_____

_____

_____

_____

_____

What can you do differently to make your limitations limit-less?

_____

_____

_____

_____

_____

Rewrite your intention from a negative to a positive.

_____

_____

_____

_____

_____

Rule #26: Own It

Failure isn't fun. There are numerous times that I've made some awful choices. Sometimes my choices were based on emotions and I failed to see the ramifications of my behavior at the time. As kids we point fingers, blame others, and make excuses for screwing up. Sadly, as adults, many of us do the same thing. We punish others as we sink, holding them hostage to our own irresponsibility.

Making mistakes is a part of growth. The way we learn is from reevaluating our actions to glean information that can benefit us or others. It is ok to grieve over those decisions that cost us nights of peace and sleep. At some point, the grieving ends and we must accept responsibility.

I am proud of my dear friend Nate. He hasn't always made the best of choices, yet, he has taken ownership of his mess which has allowed him to be transparent and authentic in his relationships. Owning it is about taking responsibility. It is accepting faults but not staying in the space. It is choosing to learn from your mistakes and doing something different. Otherwise, we contaminate our surroundings with baggage that weighs us down. The lesson continues to return until we are able to discern and do something that will elevate us to the next level.

ACTION POINT

I love the image of emotional baggage.
Let's unpack your bags…

What are you carrying that needs to be re-
moved and released? Make a list of all of the
gage that you need to let go including those you need to forgive.

_____

_____

_____

_____

_____

Forgiveness isn't about the other person. It is about you!

Rule #27: Tune Out Negativity

I recently had breakfast with a dear friend I haven't seen in a few years, As always, our conversations are centered around our families, work life, and the relationships that connect us to our reality. As she began to share, I found myself elated about her life changes and the promotion on her job. When it became my turn to share, she became overly concerned. Her questions were more about my child. Is she ok with your travel? How is she adjusting? She then asked about my husband–a similar line of questions followed. Did he mind my travel? I began to feel as if I was being interrogated by a benevolent dictator.

What initially began as a dialogue became a trial of my ability to parent effectively. At the time, I wasn't as quick witted because I was taken aback. I was not expecting this and it was shocking. I can't apologize for my life and who I am.

I was blessed to visit with a very prominent woman I admire, respect, and genuinely like. At dinner one night, Rita listened as I recapped the conversation with my friend. Rita travels often. This divorced mother is a national leader who impacts the lives of people around the world. She said several things that were profound.

First, everyone isn't wired the same way. I realized at that moment we are different beyond the usual suspects–gender, race, class. We are designed differently to accomplish different tasks. From our birth, God had a plan for each of us down to our gender, race, location, etc. to fulfill a purpose. Often, we view others through our limited lens. If we believe it, we then believe others can achieve it. We place our limitations on others because we don't see the possibility in ourselves. I'm sure many children could have reached their goals if they didn't have voices in their lives that tell them what they cannot do instead of encouraging them to try.

My friend meant no harm. I don't think she was being malicious. I have had others who guise jealousy under a mask of concern. It reminded me of Rita's second point–get friends who understand. It is painful to clean our closet of companions. Like the dress size ten that we know we'll never slide into because our hips have found comfort on us, we hang on too long. The sooner we move that dress, we open up space for a better fit, a compliment to who we are can now reside in that space.

There is a scripture that basically states we all have gifts and some are more prevalent because it is in proportion to our faith. I have met singers who are comparable to stars like Beyoncé. The difference as to why one is a celebrity and another is not can be attributed to a number of factors. For some, it is the fact they didn't pursue their gift and allowed naysayers to persuade them to do otherwise. Your faith in yourself and your ability is critical to your success.

If it is time to rid yourself of negative thoughts, friends, or other toxic relationships that impede your progress, it is time to let it go! The only thing in the way of you being who you were designed to be is you. Stop making comparisons to others–limiting your own possibilities because of negativity.

ACTION POINT

What are the toxic relationships in your life?
How are these relationships hurting you?

_____

_____

_____

_____

_____

How are they keeping you from being your best self?

_____

_____

_____

_____

If you could replace the negativity in your life, what would take its place?

_____

_____

_____

_____

_____

Rule #28: If It Hurts, Handle It.

I was always told, "No pain, no gain." I remember dealing with a number of injuries when I would overextend myself while exercising. I thought I was doing something good, going beyond my limits toward what was perceived as progress. In the end, I spent more time recovering from that bad decision than I actually did working out. As I write this now, my knee hurts. In the past, my lack of recognition of the pain resulted in knee surgery. I continued to put weight on the knee, climbing stairs even when I felt the excruciating pain of bone rubbing against bone creating an indescribable friction that required pain medicine to sedate it temporarily.

That analogy represents what we all do. We find temporary fixes that subdue us from really dealing with the reality we are presented. We push through it. We ignore the signs until we can no longer tolerate it. For some of us, our lack of attention to those messages can immobilize us and even place us at the doorstep of death.

My unwillingness to listen previously kept me off work for months because it resulted in an unavoidable surgery. I was so dedicated to a job that when I calculated my salary with the hours I worked I was giving more to them than it was providing me. My father would always say I should just work at MacDonald's because my hourly wage was comparable when I was putting in six days. The job went on while I was home healing.

Sometimes the very thing we are trying to maintain is what keeps us from moving. I believe my emotional and psychological strain from that overtaxing position manifested itself in my body. My knee was a cry out for the overwhelming load I was carrying. My knee today is a reminder. This time, I won't wait to respond. When it hurts, don't self-diagnose with meds like food, sex, work, or bad relationships because when the dose is done, the pain resumes and often is compounded with other ailments. Deal with it and if you need to lift weight to get release, remove the obstacle.

ACTION POINT

What hurts physically?

_____

_____

_____

_____

_____

Is there an emotional correlation to the pain?

_____

_____

_____

_____

_____

What are your meds? What is it that you use to treat your pain? - Sex? Alcohol? Work? Shopping?

_____

_____

_____

_____

What do you do to avoid what is really happening?

_____

_____

_____

_____

_____

Write a letter to the pain. Address what keeps you from being whole and well. If the pain is a person or situation, reflect on how it started, where things took a turn and how you need to make things well.

Rule #29: Watch Where Your Time Goes – That's What You Value

As a Christian, the Bible has been a guide for me. I can't say I've followed all of it. Some things I've even avoided or ran from them because I wanted to do things my way which resulted in disaster. I was amazed at Christ and his relationship with his Father, God. I couldn't do everything I should and yet, Christ made it a point to be obedient. I realized his constant communication through prayer was a significant part of his time. It was the use of time well spent that gave him the power to endure the trials and tribulations he faced. He looked like God because he spent time in the presence of God.

When I reflect on my relationship with my mother, I don't physically look like her but as soon as I talk or you see my mannerisms it is obvious you are in the presence of Dorothy Jean's daughter. The same applies with my twelve year old mini-me. Although she resembles me in appearance, her demeanor is much like mine. She is quick witted, silly, and introspective (like her dad). She acts like us because her time is spent with us. The lesson for each of us is that we are not only a reflection of our families but our environments mold us as well.

I knew a lady who was a vegetarian but when we saw her eating, she always seemed to snack on cakes and pies. She also struggled with weight issues. So often we say we are filling ourselves with healthy foods but in actuality we are eating snacks that make us feel good but harm us. It is imperative to think about how our environments feed us. What are you eating or better yet, what is eating you?

ACTION POINT

What are you feeding yourself?

_____

_____

_____

_____

_____

Is it positive people that will take you where you want to go?

_____

_____

_____

_____

_____

Or are you returning to the old habits that keep you from creating the change you wish to see?

_____

_____

_____

_____

_____

Final Thoughts

One of my greatest contributions to the planet is my daughter, Kazai. She teaches me daily the importance of relating. No matter how great my intentions might be, if my daughter doesn't connect, the ideas and lessons I share are fruitless.

I have spent years building a foundation of trust and openness, hoping that even in my moments of vulnerability we have the ability to move forward. It isn't easy. I disappoint her and there are times she has disappointed me. It doesn't matter. The relationship we share is critical and I will do what I can to have a connection with my daughter. I appreciate her strengths and those areas that challenge her.

She has taught me that my full love of who she is as a person allows me to love myself fully. There is no mess up that she can do that will change how I feel about her. As we share stories, I learn of her dreams, ambitions and difficulties. I will always be available to listen, to hear, and understand her story and how it connects to my own.

It is the story that connects us. The story evolves and is always adding new characters, situations, and paths to take. The story is important.

I also realized that when I brought together the amazing women for my research group that I would be changed by their stories. As women, we spend so much time helping others create their stories that we do not take time to reflect on our own stories. We keep moving and moving, failing to see the lessons learned that resulted in our growth. We so often focus on the hurt that we seldom witness the amount of healing. Those elements are all a part of reflecting and revisiting the story of our lives.

This book is designed to allow you to simmer in those moments of your journey. There are no right or wrong answers. But it is an opportunity to take an inventory of where you have been, where you want to go, and evaluate the gaps that exist between the two. In doing so, you will be more authentic and create more relationships that are transparent and transformational.

In my research, I have read numerous articles that demonstrate that social capital in the lives of women is often used in our personal circles and not as much to build our professional goals. I am hoping that this book will drive women to building relationships with others that support both areas. We need personal relationships that help us with dealing with emotional well-being, but we also need each other to share information that will support our professional dreams. Our opportunities to do this are limited often because of our busy schedules. Our circles typically look like us and this limits us from obtaining a unique perspective that can enrich and even challenge our comfortable lives. It is especially important that diverse groups of women come together to enlighten and inform one another. Operating in silos will only take us so far.

I recently held a screening of a documentary I participated in entitled *Friendly Captivity*, which was about the voyage of seven women from Dallas visiting India. Visiting southern India with a group of strangers who were so different than me was a huge risk taking moment in my life but also one that began my quest to empowering women. It was there that the seeds for creating safe spaces for dialogue around tough issues with women took root in my spirit.

Nevertheless, those who attended the screening enjoyed the opportunity to dialogue and appreciated the chance to connect with diverse women. The women remarked that they wished there were more opportunities for these safe spaces to relate. It is my desire to help women from different backgrounds connect and build strong networks that change our lives, our communities, and our world. I find that we have more in common with each other than we think. We all worry about many of the same things and when given the chance to break down those walls that keep us apart we can build strong, lasting friendships.

We have allowed fear to paralyze us from connecting. When I look at my daughter and I see the world that she is moving into as a young woman, she has to be educated and have work related experience to be successful but also she has to know how to navigate the world of relationships at work, at home, and in the community. She will need tools that will help her beyond a textbook on building advocates and allies in an ever changing world. So much media lately has been instrumental in creating this "us versus them" syndrome. We are afraid of one another. Women fight on television as if it is commonplace to throw drinks in another's face. The level of disrespect to one another is huge and at some point, this has to stop.

The voices of women are needed in so many areas and leadership is lacking because we are not at the table. It will be imperative that we connect and raise daughters as well as sons who will have an appreciation for the differences that exist in each other. We will not change the world until we begin to look at ourselves deeply and share our learning with one another. Putnam's book, *Bowling Alone*, reveals that in communities that have high social capital, child well-being, education, and civic engagement are stronger. In communities that have low social capital, often there is a higher crime rate as well as other social ills. The need to connect is paramount to our changing society and I want to empower women to begin this journey with me to dig deep, discover, and dialogue.

I hope this book is the beginning of your journey. I am currently using Kegan and Lahey's work on *Immunity to Change* to begin working with women to determine the barriers that keep us from creating the lives we desire that impact our personal and professional lies. My dissertation work will be around this topic and I will evaluate the role of our social networks in creating change. It is my desire to evaluate how women view one another and if these perceptions impact our ability to build diverse networks. If you are interested in being involved at a greater level through individual or group work, feel free to reach out to join this growing network of learners!

About the Author

Froswa' Booker-Drew

Experience combined with education has prepared Froswa' for building a diverse network of individuals and organizations around the world. Froswa' Booker-Drew has more than 20 years of experience in leadership development, training, nonprofit management, education and social services. She currently is employed by *World Vision*, US Programs serving as Community Youth Development Director for the Southeastern United States managing staff and programs across the region.

In addition, Froswa' is an instructor in the Nonprofit Certificate Program at UT-Arlington and has provided consulting services to a number of nonprofits around the country including...

- AWOW International
- Girls Leadership Initiative (US & Ghana)
- Texas Association of Nonprofit Organizations
- Texas Council on Family Violence
- Texas Muslim Women's Foundation
- International Visitors Council—Dallas
- Mothers & More (IL)

- Prime Time Sister Circles (DC)
- Girls Inc—Tarrant County
- Dallas Women's Foundation

She has worked with three national nonprofits in administrative roles providing capacity building to congregations, educational organizations, and municipalities. Froswa' has also been an instructor at several colleges such as Jarvis Christian College and Southwestern Christian College and serves as a guest lecturer at the University of North Texas at Dallas. She is also a grant reviewer for several federal agencies and foundations.

Booker-Drew is a graduate from Oklahoma City University with a Master of Liberal Arts in Humanities. She received her undergraduate degree from the University of Texas at Arlington in History. As a student, she was extremely involved in campus and community activities.

Currently, Froswa' is in her third year of doctoral studies in Leadership and Change at Antioch University in Yellow Springs, Ohio.

Froswa's focus is on building social capital in individuals and organizations. She has served as a Board Member of the *Texas Association of Nonprofit Organizations* and is currently involved with *Girls Inc—Tarrant County* as a member of the Director's Circle.

Booker-Drew was a part of the documentary, *Friendly Captivity*, a film that follows a cast of seven women from Dallas to India in 2008. Because of this experience, she has dedicated much of her spare time to identifying ways to support organizations that address vulnerable and marginalized youth.

Froswa' received the 2009 Woman of the Year Award by *Zeta Phi Beta Sorority, Inc.* and was awarded Diversity Ambassador for the *American Red Cross*. She is a trainer for a number of organizations such as *Women Empowering Girls*

Network and offers coaching through *Foundation Coaching.* Much of her training includes topics such as change management, social capital, authentic and transformational leadership for women.

Froswa' was awarded 2012 Outstanding African American Alumni from the University of Texas at Arlington and was a 2012 semi-finalist for the SMU TED Talks.